DATA SCIENCE FOR BEGINNERS

Your Guide to Understanding and
Using Data Like a Pro

MAXWELL RIVERS

INTRODUCTION

Welcome to "Data Science for Beginners," your passport to the world of data science, regardless of your prior experience or technical background.

Imagine being able to extract valuable insights from numbers, make well-informed decisions, and create groundbreaking solutions that impact industries and communities. Data science empowers you to do just that, and this book is your compass on this remarkable journey.

Why Data Science Matters

Data science is the modern-day alchemy, transforming raw data into goldmines of knowledge. Whether you're a student on a quest for wisdom, a professional eager to unlock new career possibilities, or simply a curious soul seeking to decipher the digital enigma, this book is your gateway to the incredible world of data science.

What Awaits You

Within these pages, we demystify complex concepts and guide you through the world of data science. Each chapter is an expedition, starting from the basics and venturing into data collection, analysis, and machine learning.

Whether you aim to advance your career, conquer exciting projects, or merely satisfy your curiosity, "Data Science for Beginners" is your key to unlocking the secrets of data.

CONTENTS

CHAPTER 1: GETTING STARTED WITH DATA SCIENCE

1.1 The Data Science Lifecycle

Data science is not just a collection of techniques and tools; it's a systematic approach to solving complex problems using data. At its core is the data science lifecycle, a structured framework that guides the process of turning raw data into actionable insights. This lifecycle provides a roadmap for data scientists, helping them navigate the various stages of a data-driven project.

The Stages of the Data Science Lifecycle:

1. **Problem Formulation:** Every data science project begins with a question or a problem. In this initial stage, you define the problem you want to solve and set clear objectives. For example, you might ask, "Can we predict customer churn?" or "How can we optimize our supply chain?"
2. **Data Collection:** Once you've framed your problem, you need data to work with. Data can come from various sources, such as databases, sensors, surveys, or web scraping. It's crucial to gather relevant and high-quality data for your analysis.
3. **Data Cleaning and Preprocessing:** Raw data is often messy, incomplete, or inconsistent. Data cleaning involves removing errors, handling missing values, and ensuring data quality. Data

preprocessing includes tasks like normalization, transformation, and feature engineering to prepare the data for analysis.

4. **Exploratory Data Analysis (EDA):** In this stage, you explore the data to understand its characteristics, patterns, and relationships. Data visualization is a powerful tool here, helping you uncover insights and potential outliers.

5. **Model Building:** With a clear understanding of the data, you can start building models. Machine learning algorithms and statistical methods are used to create models that can make predictions, classify data, or uncover hidden patterns.

6. **Evaluation:** Once you've built your models, it's essential to evaluate their performance. Different metrics and techniques are used to assess how well your models are doing. This step helps you fine-tune your models and select the best one for your problem.

7. **Deployment:** The insights and models you've developed need to be put into action. Deployment involves integrating your findings into a practical solution, whether it's a recommendation system, a predictive tool, or a data-driven decision-making process.

8. **Monitoring and Maintenance:** Data science doesn't end with deployment. Models and solutions require ongoing monitoring to ensure they remain effective and accurate. You may need to update models as new data becomes available or as the problem evolves.

9. **Communication:** Effective communication is a crucial aspect of the data science lifecycle. You need to convey your findings, insights, and recommendations to stakeholders, which may include non-technical audiences. Visualization and storytelling play a key role here.

Iterative Nature of the Lifecycle:

It's important to note that the data science lifecycle is often iterative. You may find that as you progress through the stages, you need to revisit previous steps based on new insights or changes in your problem statement. This iterative approach allows data scientists to adapt to evolving circumstances and continuously improve their solutions.

In essence, the data science lifecycle is your roadmap to transforming data into actionable knowledge. It's the foundation upon which data science projects are built, and understanding its stages is the first step towards becoming a proficient data scientist. In the chapters ahead, we'll explore each stage in more detail, equipping you with the skills and knowledge to navigate this exciting journey.

1.2 Tools and Software

In the world of data science, tools and software are the instruments that empower you to turn data into insights, models, and actionable decisions. They are the digital companions on your data-driven journey, and choosing the right ones is a critical step in your quest for success. In this section, we'll explore some of the essential tools and software commonly used in the field of data science.

1. Programming Languages:

Python: Python is the undisputed king of programming languages in data science. Its simplicity, versatility, and a rich ecosystem of libraries make it the go-to choice for data scientists. Libraries like NumPy, pandas, Matplotlib, and scikit-learn provide the necessary tools for data manipulation, analysis, and machine learning.

R: R is another powerful programming language specifically designed for statistical computing and data analysis. It excels in data visualization and statistical modeling. Data scientists often choose R for its extensive collection of packages tailored to data analysis.

SQL: SQL (Structured Query Language) is essential for managing and querying relational databases. It's a crucial skill for retrieving and preprocessing data from database systems.

2. Integrated Development Environments (IDEs):

Jupyter Notebook: Jupyter Notebook is a popular choice for interactive data analysis and visualization. It allows you to combine code, visualizations, and explanatory text in a single document, making it ideal for sharing insights with others.

Spyder: Spyder is an open-source IDE designed specifically for data science. It offers an interactive environment for data exploration and analysis, with built-in support for libraries like NumPy and pandas.

RStudio: If you're working with R, RStudio is a dedicated IDE that provides an integrated environment for R programming, data visualization, and report generation.

3. Data Visualization Tools:

Matplotlib: Matplotlib is a widely used Python library for creating static, animated, and interactive visualizations. It's highly customizable and suitable for a wide range of plotting needs.

Seaborn: Seaborn is built on top of Matplotlib and is designed for creating attractive and informative statistical graphics. It simplifies many aspects of data visualization.

Tableau: Tableau is a powerful data visualization tool that allows you to create interactive and shareable dashboards. It's a favorite among business analysts and data professionals for its ease of use.

4. Machine Learning Libraries:

scikit-learn: scikit-learn is a comprehensive machine learning library for Python. It provides tools for classification, regression, clustering, and more, along with model selection and evaluation functions.

TensorFlow and PyTorch: These libraries are essential for deep learning and neural network development. They offer flexibility and scalability for building complex machine learning models.

5. Data Wrangling and Analysis:

pandas: pandas is a Python library for data manipulation and analysis. It provides data structures like DataFrames and Series, making it easy to clean, transform, and explore data.

Databases: Tools for working with databases like PostgreSQL, MySQL, and MongoDB are crucial for data storage, retrieval, and management.

6. Big Data Technologies:

Hadoop: Apache Hadoop is an open-source framework for distributed storage and processing of large datasets. It's used in big data applications where traditional databases may not suffice.

Apache Spark: Apache Spark is a powerful data processing engine that simplifies big data analytics. It offers high-level APIs in languages like Python and Scala and supports real-time data processing.

7. Version Control:

Git: Git is essential for tracking changes in your code and collaborating with others. Platforms like GitHub and GitLab provide hosting and collaboration features.

8. Cloud Services:

Amazon Web Services (AWS), Google Cloud Platform (GCP), Microsoft Azure: These cloud platforms offer scalable computing resources and a wide range of data science tools and services, making it easier to work with large datasets and deploy models.

The choice of tools and software depends on your specific project, preferences, and the resources available to you. It's common for data scientists to use a combination of these tools to address various aspects of a project. Remember that proficiency with these tools will develop over time, so don't be discouraged if you're just starting out. Your understanding of these tools will deepen as you gain experience in the field of data science.

1.3 Setting Up Your Data Science Environment

Now that you've gained a glimpse of the data science landscape and the essential tools at your disposal, it's time to roll up your sleeves and create your data science environment. This environment will serve as your digital workspace, where you'll explore data, write code, build models, and conduct analyses. Setting it up correctly is crucial for a smooth and productive data science journey.

1. Choose Your Programming Language:

At the heart of your data science environment lies your choice of programming language. Python, R, and SQL are the most common languages used in data science. Python, in particular, is highly recommended for its versatility and extensive libraries for data manipulation, analysis, and machine learning.

2. Install Python and Libraries:

If you've opted for Python, start by installing it on your computer. You can download Python from the official website (python.org) and follow the installation instructions. Once Python is installed, use the package manager pip to install essential libraries such as NumPy, pandas, Matplotlib, and scikit-learn. You can do this by running commands like:

```
pip install numpy pandas matplotlib scikit-learn
```

3. Set Up an Integrated Development Environment (IDE):

An Integrated Development Environment (IDE) provides a user-friendly interface for writing and running code. Jupyter Notebook is a fantastic choice for data science projects due to its interactivity and support for combining code, visualizations, and explanations in one document. Install Jupyter Notebook using pip:

```
pip install jupyter
```

To start a Jupyter Notebook, open your terminal or command prompt and run:

```
jupyter notebook
```

This will launch a web-based interface where you can create and manage notebooks.

4. Version Control with Git:

Version control is crucial for tracking changes in your code and collaborating with others. Install Git on your machine and set up a Git repository for your data science projects. Platforms like GitHub or GitLab offer hosting and collaboration features.

5. Explore Cloud Services:

While setting up a local environment is essential, you should also consider using cloud services like Amazon Web Services (AWS), Google Cloud Platform (GCP), or Microsoft Azure. Cloud platforms provide scalable computing resources and a range of pre-configured data science tools and services. They can be especially useful for handling large datasets and running computationally intensive tasks.

6. Data Storage and Databases:

If your project involves working with databases, install and configure database management systems like PostgreSQL, MySQL, or MongoDB as needed. You'll also want to explore Python libraries for database connections, such as SQLAlchemy or pymongo.

7. Explore Virtual Environments:

Virtual environments help you manage dependencies and isolate project-specific packages. Python provides the venv module for creating virtual environments. Using virtual environments ensures that your data science projects remain separate and avoid conflicts between libraries.

8. Documentation and Collaboration:

Consider using tools like Jupyter Notebook, which allows you to document your code and findings in a format that's easy to share with others. Collaborative platforms like JupyterHub, Google Colab, or even GitHub offer features for collaborative coding and documentation.

9. Continuous Learning:

The data science field is ever-evolving. As you set up your environment, make a commitment to continuous learning. Follow blogs, online courses, and join data science communities to stay updated on the latest developments and best practices.

CHAPTER 2: DATA ACQUISITION

2.1 Data Sources

Data, in its various forms, can be found in numerous places, each offering unique opportunities and challenges. To become a proficient data scientist, you must familiarize yourself with these sources and learn how to navigate their intricacies.

Common Data Sources:

1. **Databases:** Structured data often resides in relational databases, which are organized into tables with rows and columns. Popular database management systems include MySQL, PostgreSQL, SQL Server, and Oracle. Data scientists use SQL queries to retrieve, manipulate, and analyze data from these sources.
2. **Files:** Data can be stored in various file formats such as CSV, Excel spreadsheets, JSON, XML, and more. These files are accessible with programming languages like Python, R, and libraries like pandas.
3. **Web Data:** The internet is a treasure trove of data. Web scraping allows you to extract information from websites and web pages. This technique is invaluable for collecting data from sources like news articles, social media, e-commerce sites, and public APIs (Application Programming Interfaces).

4. **Sensor Data:** In the age of IoT (Internet of Things), sensors collect vast amounts of data from devices and systems. This data can include temperature readings, GPS coordinates, environmental metrics, and more. Analyzing sensor data is crucial in fields like environmental science, healthcare, and manufacturing.

5. **Logs and Clickstream Data:** Logs generated by applications, websites, and servers record user interactions and system events. Analyzing these logs provides insights into user behavior, performance issues, and security threats.

6. **Social Media Data:** Social media platforms generate an enormous volume of data through user interactions, posts, comments, and likes. This data is valuable for sentiment analysis, trend prediction, and understanding user preferences.

7. **Text and Documents:** Unstructured text data, such as articles, reports, and emails, contains valuable information. Natural Language Processing (NLP) techniques are used to analyze and extract insights from text data.

8. **Images and Videos:** Visual data, including images and videos, is analyzed using computer vision techniques. This data source has applications in fields like healthcare (medical imaging), autonomous vehicles, and security.

9. **Historical Data:** Historical records and archives provide a rich source of data for research, trend analysis, and historical context. Libraries, museums, and government agencies often maintain historical data repositories.

Challenges in Data Acquisition:

While these data sources offer a wealth of information, data acquisition comes with its set of challenges:

1. **Data Quality:** Data may contain errors, inconsistencies, or missing values. Ensuring data quality is a critical aspect of data acquisition.

2. **Data Privacy and Ethics:** Gathering and using data must be done in compliance with privacy laws and ethical considerations. Sensitive data must be handled with care and in accordance with relevant regulations.

3. **Data Volume:** Some data sources, particularly sensor data and social media streams, can produce massive volumes of data. Storage, processing, and analysis of big data require specialized tools and infrastructure.
4. **Data Integration:** In real-world scenarios, data often comes from multiple sources with different formats and structures. Integrating this data can be a complex task.
5. **Data Access:** Some data sources may have access restrictions or require permissions. Accessing data legally and ethically is essential.

Understanding the various data sources and their characteristics is the first step in the data acquisition process. Depending on your project's goals and requirements, you'll need to choose the appropriate sources, design data collection strategies, and apply data cleaning and preprocessing techniques to prepare the data for analysis.

2.2 Collecting Data

Once you've identified the potential data sources for your data science project, the next crucial step is collecting the data. Data collection involves systematically gathering information from various sources, ensuring its accuracy, and storing it in a format suitable for analysis. This phase is the foundation upon which the rest of your data science journey is built.

Data Collection Methods:

1. **Manual Entry:** For small-scale projects, you can manually input data from sources like printed documents or surveys into digital formats. While this method is straightforward, it can be time-consuming and prone to human errors.
2. **Web Scraping:** Web scraping is the automated extraction of data from websites and web pages. It involves using specialized tools and libraries to navigate web content and gather relevant information. Web scraping is invaluable for collecting data from online sources such as news sites, e-commerce platforms, and social media.

3. **APIs (Application Programming Interfaces):** Many online services and platforms offer APIs that allow you to programmatically access and retrieve data. APIs provide structured and up-to-date data, making them a reliable source for real-time information.

4. **Sensor Data Acquisition:** In IoT and environmental monitoring, data is collected from sensors placed in physical devices and environments. These sensors capture various types of data, including temperature, humidity, GPS coordinates, and more.

5. **Database Queries:** When working with structured data stored in databases, you can use SQL queries to retrieve specific datasets or tables. This method is common when dealing with data from corporate databases.

6. **Logs and Clickstream Data:** Data generated by applications, websites, and servers is often logged. Analyzing logs and clickstream data can provide insights into user behavior, application performance, and security incidents.

7. **Surveys and Questionnaires:** Surveys and questionnaires are tools for collecting data directly from individuals or groups. This method is widely used in social sciences, market research, and public opinion analysis.

Best Practices in Data Collection:

1. **Define Data Requirements:** Before collecting data, clearly define the data you need for your analysis. Establish data collection criteria, including data types, formats, and quality standards.

2. **Data Privacy and Ethics:** Respect data privacy and ethical considerations. If collecting personal or sensitive data, ensure compliance with relevant laws and regulations, such as GDPR (General Data Protection Regulation) or HIPAA (Health Insurance Portability and Accountability Act).

3. **Data Sampling:** In some cases, collecting all available data may be impractical or unnecessary. Sampling involves selecting a representative subset of data for analysis. It can save time and resources while providing accurate insights.

4. **Automate Data Collection:** Whenever possible, automate data collection processes using scripts or tools. Automation reduces the risk of human errors and ensures data consistency.
5. **Data Validation:** Implement data validation checks during collection to identify and correct errors early in the process. Validation helps maintain data accuracy and integrity.
6. **Document Data Sources:** Keep detailed records of data sources, collection methods, and any transformations applied to the data. Documentation is crucial for reproducibility and transparency in data science projects.
7. **Data Storage:** Choose an appropriate data storage solution based on the volume and format of your data. Ensure data security and implement backup strategies to prevent data loss.
8. **Data Cleansing:** After data collection, perform data cleaning and preprocessing to address missing values, outliers, and inconsistencies. Clean, high-quality data is essential for meaningful analysis.

Effective data collection sets the stage for robust data analysis and modeling. It allows you to work with reliable, relevant data that can lead to valuable insights and informed decision-making.

2.3 Data Formats

In the world of data science, data comes in various formats, each with its own structure and characteristics. Understanding different data formats is essential because it influences how you collect, store, preprocess, and analyze data. In this section, we'll explore some common data formats encountered in data science.

1. Tabular Data (Structured Data):

Description: Tabular data is organized in rows and columns, much like a spreadsheet. Each row represents a single observation, and each column represents a variable or attribute. This format is highly structured and is commonly used in databases and CSV files.

Use Cases: Tabular data is suitable for storing data with a clear structure, such as sales records, customer information, and financial data.

Tools: Libraries like pandas in Python and data frames in R are well-suited for working with tabular data.

2. JSON (JavaScript Object Notation):

Description: JSON is a lightweight, text-based data format that is easy for both humans and machines to read. It uses a key-value pair structure and can represent complex data hierarchies. JSON is commonly used for web APIs and configuration files.

Use Cases: JSON is often used to exchange data between a web server and a web client, making it a popular choice for data transfer on the internet.

Tools: Most programming languages have libraries or built-in functions for parsing and generating JSON data.

3. XML (Extensible Markup Language):

Description: XML is another text-based data format used for structuring data hierarchically. It uses tags to define elements and their attributes. XML is commonly used for document storage and data interchange.

Use Cases: XML is prevalent in industries like finance, healthcare, and government, where structured data storage and exchange are critical.

Tools: Many programming languages have libraries for parsing XML, such as Python's xml.etree.ElementTree and Java's javax.xml package.

4. CSV (Comma-Separated Values):

Description: CSV is a simple text-based format for representing tabular data. Data values are separated by commas (or other delimiters like semicolons or tabs). It is widely used because of its simplicity.

Use Cases: CSV files are commonly used for data exchange and storage when a structured, tabular format is required.

Tools: Virtually all programming languages provide libraries or functions for reading and writing CSV files.

5. Text Data:

Description: Text data consists of unstructured text, which can be in the form of documents, articles, social media posts, emails, and more. Text data is often challenging to work with due to its lack of structure.

Use Cases: Text data is valuable for natural language processing (NLP) tasks such as sentiment analysis, text classification, and information extraction.

Tools: NLP libraries like NLTK (Natural Language Toolkit) for Python and the tm package in R are commonly used for text data analysis.

6. Binary Data:

Description: Binary data is composed of sequences of 0s and 1s and is not human-readable. It is used for various purposes, including encoding images, audio files, and serialized objects.

Use Cases: Binary data is essential for storing and transmitting multimedia files, machine learning models, and binary protocols.

Tools: Working with binary data often requires specialized libraries or functions, depending on the specific data type.

7. Image and Video Data:

Description: Image and video data represent visual information. Images can be in formats like JPEG, PNG, or BMP, while video data may use formats like MP4 or AVI.

Use Cases: Image and video data are used in computer vision tasks, medical imaging, surveillance, and multimedia applications.

Tools: Libraries like OpenCV (Open Source Computer Vision Library) in Python are commonly used for working with image and video data.

Each data format has its own advantages and limitations, and choosing the right format depends on the nature of your data and the tasks you need to perform. As a data scientist, your ability to work with diverse data formats is a valuable skill that enables you to extract insights and knowledge from a wide range of sources.

2.4 Data Cleaning and Preprocessing

Data, in its raw form, is often far from ready for analysis. It's like a rough diamond that needs polishing to reveal its true value. Data cleaning and preprocessing are the crucial steps that transform raw data into a usable and reliable format for analysis. These steps involve identifying and rectifying errors, handling missing values, and preparing the data for further exploration and modeling.

Why Data Cleaning and Preprocessing are Essential:

1. **Ensuring Data Quality:** Raw data can contain errors, inconsistencies, and inaccuracies. Data cleaning helps improve data quality, making it more reliable for analysis.
2. **Enhancing Analysis:** Preprocessed data is easier to work with and can lead to more accurate and meaningful insights. It eliminates noise and irrelevant information.
3. **Handling Missing Values:** Datasets often have missing values, which can impact the validity of analyses. Preprocessing involves strategies for handling missing data, such as imputation or removal.

4. **Standardizing Data:** Data collected from various sources may have different units or scales. Standardization ensures that data is in a consistent format for analysis.

Common Data Cleaning and Preprocessing Techniques:

1. **Handling Missing Data:**
   o **Imputation:** Replace missing values with estimated or calculated values based on available data. Techniques include mean imputation, median imputation, or using machine learning models for imputation.
   o **Removal:** If the missing values are too numerous or cannot be reasonably imputed, you may choose to remove rows or columns with missing data.
2. **Outlier Detection and Treatment:**
   o **Identify Outliers:** Use statistical methods or visualization techniques to detect outliers in the data.
   o **Treatment:** Decide whether to remove outliers, transform them, or treat them separately based on domain knowledge.
3. **Data Transformation:**
   o **Normalization:** Scaling data to have a common scale (e.g., between 0 and 1) to mitigate the impact of varying units.
   o **Log Transformation:** Useful for data that follows a skewed distribution, making it more normally distributed.
4. **Encoding Categorical Data:**
   o Convert categorical variables (non-numeric) into numerical format for analysis. Techniques include one-hot encoding and label encoding.
5. **Handling Duplicates:**
   o Identify and remove duplicate records or rows to prevent data redundancy.
6. **Feature Selection:**
   o Choose relevant features (variables) for analysis to reduce dimensionality and improve model performance.
7. **Data Splitting:**
   o Divide data into training, validation, and test sets for model development and evaluation.
8. **Dealing with Time Series Data:**

- o Time series data often requires special handling, such as resampling, smoothing, or windowing.
9. **Addressing Skewed Data:**
   - o For imbalanced datasets, employ techniques like oversampling, undersampling, or synthetic data generation.

Challenges in Data Cleaning and Preprocessing:

- **Complexity:** Data preprocessing can be a complex and iterative process, especially when dealing with large and messy datasets.
- **Data Integrity:** Overzealous cleaning can remove valid information, so it's crucial to balance cleaning with maintaining data integrity.
- **Resource Intensive:** Depending on the dataset's size and complexity, data preprocessing can require significant computational resources.

Data cleaning and preprocessing are often seen as the less glamorous aspects of data science, but they are foundational to the success of any data analysis or modeling project. Without these critical steps, the results of your analysis could be compromised, leading to inaccurate conclusions and decisions.

CHAPTER 3: EXPLORATORY DATA ANALYSIS

3.1 Understanding Your Data

Before you can extract meaningful insights from data, you must first understand an initial step. This initial step, often referred to as data exploration, is a pivotal part of the data analysis process. It involves getting acquainted with your dataset, grasping its structure, and uncovering the initial nuances that will guide your subsequent analyses.

The Importance of Understanding Your Data:

1. **Contextual Awareness:** Understanding the context in which the data was collected is crucial. Without context, you may misinterpret the data and draw incorrect conclusions.
2. **Identifying Data Types:** Different types of data (e.g., numerical, categorical, text) require different analysis techniques. Understanding the data types in your dataset helps you choose appropriate methods.
3. **Spotting Anomalies:** Early data exploration can reveal anomalies, outliers, and errors that need attention. Identifying these issues at the outset can save time and prevent erroneous results.

4. **Formulating Hypotheses:** As you explore the data, you may develop hypotheses or questions about patterns, relationships, or trends that warrant further investigation.

Methods of Understanding Your Data:

1. **Descriptive Statistics:** Start by calculating basic descriptive statistics like mean, median, standard deviation, and quartiles. These measures provide an initial overview of the data's central tendency, spread, and distribution.
2. **Data Visualization:** Visualizations are powerful tools for understanding data. Create histograms, box plots, scatter plots, and bar charts to explore the distribution and relationships within your data. Visualization tools like Matplotlib (Python) or ggplot2 (R) can be immensely helpful.
3. **Summary Tables:** Generate summary tables to examine categorical data. These tables can provide insights into the frequency and distribution of different categories.
4. **Correlation Analysis:** Explore relationships between variables by calculating correlation coefficients. This helps identify potential dependencies and associations in the data.
5. **Data Profiling:** Data profiling tools and techniques help you understand the data's structure, including the presence of missing values, duplicates, and unique identifiers.
6. **Domain Knowledge:** Leverage your domain expertise or collaborate with subject matter experts who can provide valuable insights into the data and its potential quirks.

Key Questions to Ask:

1. **What does each variable represent?** Understand the meaning and relevance of each variable in your dataset.
2. **What is the data's distribution?** Examine the distribution of numerical variables to identify patterns and outliers.
3. **Are there missing values?** Determine the extent of missing data and consider strategies for handling it.
4. **Do variables exhibit correlations or patterns?** Explore relationships between variables to uncover potential insights.

5. **Are there any unusual or unexpected observations?** Look for anomalies or data points that deviate significantly from the norm.

Iterative Process: Understanding your data is not a one-time task; it's an iterative process. As you progress in your analysis, you may return to the data exploration phase to refine your understanding and generate new hypotheses.

3.2 Data Visualization

Data visualization is the art and science of representing data graphically. It is a fundamental tool in the data science toolkit, allowing you to transform raw data into visual representations that are easier to interpret and understand. Effective data visualization can reveal patterns, trends, outliers, and relationships within your data, making it an essential step in the exploratory data analysis (EDA) process.

Why Data Visualization Matters:

1. **Pattern Recognition:** Visualizations make it easier to identify patterns and trends in the data that might not be immediately apparent in raw numbers.
2. **Communication:** Visualizations are a powerful means of communicating insights and findings to non-technical stakeholders, making complex data more accessible.
3. **Exploration:** Visualization is an exploratory tool that helps you generate hypotheses and refine your understanding of the data.
4. **Quality Assurance:** Visualizations can reveal data quality issues, such as outliers or inconsistencies, that may require further investigation.

Types of Data Visualizations:

1. **Histograms:** Histograms display the distribution of numerical data by dividing it into intervals or bins and showing the frequency of data points in each bin.

2. **Box Plots:** Box plots provide a summary of the distribution of numerical data, showing the median, quartiles, and potential outliers.
3. **Scatter Plots:** Scatter plots depict the relationship between two numerical variables by displaying data points as dots on a two-dimensional plane.
4. **Bar Charts:** Bar charts are used to represent categorical data. They display categories on the x-axis and the corresponding values on the y-axis.
5. **Line Charts:** Line charts are ideal for showing trends over time. They connect data points with lines, making it easy to observe changes and patterns.
6. **Heatmaps:** Heatmaps are useful for visualizing relationships in large datasets, especially when dealing with matrices. They use color intensity to represent values.
7. **Pie Charts:** Pie charts display the parts of a whole, with each slice representing a portion of the total. They are suitable for illustrating composition.
8. **Violin Plots:** Violin plots combine a box plot and a kernel density estimation, providing a summary of the data distribution along with its probability density.
9. **Geospatial Maps:** Geospatial maps are used to visualize data on geographic regions. They are essential for location-based analyses and can reveal spatial patterns.

Best Practices in Data Visualization:

1. **Simplicity:** Keep visualizations simple and uncluttered to enhance clarity. Remove unnecessary elements that don't contribute to understanding.
2. **Labels and Titles:** Always provide labels for axes, data points, and legends. Include clear titles and captions to explain the purpose of the visualization.
3. **Color Choices:** Choose appropriate colors for your data points or categories. Avoid overly bright or conflicting colors that can distract from the data.
4. **Scale and Axes:** Ensure that scales and axes are appropriate for the data being represented. Misleading scales can distort interpretations.

5. **Annotations:** Use text, arrows, or shapes to annotate important features or observations in the visualization.
6. **Consistency:** Maintain consistency in visual style across multiple charts or graphs within a project to facilitate comparison.
7. **Interactivity:** For digital visualizations, consider adding interactive features that allow users to explore the data further.
8. **Testing:** Test your visualizations on a diverse audience to ensure they are interpretable by a broad range of viewers.

3.3 Descriptive Statistics

Descriptive statistics are a set of techniques used to summarize and describe the main features of a dataset. They provide a concise and informative overview of key characteristics such as central tendency, variability, and distribution. These statistics are fundamental tools in exploratory data analysis (EDA) and help data scientists gain insights into the nature of the data they are working with.

Key Descriptive Statistics:

1. **Measures of Central Tendency:**
   o **Mean (Average):** The sum of all values in a dataset divided by the number of observations. It represents the central value.
   o **Median (Middle Value):** The middle value in a dataset when it's ordered from smallest to largest. It is less affected by extreme values than the mean.
   o **Mode (Most Common Value):** The value that occurs most frequently in a dataset.
2. **Measures of Variability (Dispersion):**
   o **Range:** The difference between the maximum and minimum values in a dataset, providing a simple measure of spread.
   o **Variance:** A measure of how data points deviate from the mean. It quantifies the average squared difference between each data point and the mean.
   o **Standard Deviation:** The square root of the variance. It provides a measure of the average distance between data points and the mean. A smaller standard deviation indicates less variability.

- o **Interquartile Range (IQR):** The range between the first quartile (25th percentile) and the third quartile (75th percentile). It is a robust measure of spread that is less influenced by extreme values.
3. **Measures of Distribution:**
   - o **Histograms:** Visual representations of data distribution, divided into bins or intervals. They help visualize how data is spread across different ranges.
   - o **Skewness:** A measure of the asymmetry of the data distribution. Positive skewness indicates a longer tail on the right, while negative skewness indicates a longer tail on the left.
- o **Kurtosis:** A measure of the "tailedness" of the data distribution. High kurtosis indicates heavy tails, while low kurtosis indicates light tails.

Use Cases for Descriptive Statistics:

1. **Data Summarization:** Descriptive statistics provide a concise summary of the data, helping data scientists quickly grasp its key characteristics.
2. **Data Comparison:** Comparing the means, medians, or distributions of different datasets can reveal insights into their differences or similarities.
3. **Outlier Detection:** Measures like the range, standard deviation, and IQR can help identify outliers or extreme values in the data.
4. **Data Normalization:** Understanding the mean and standard deviation is essential when normalizing or standardizing data for modeling purposes.
5. **Data Preprocessing:** Descriptive statistics can guide decisions about how to handle missing values, impute data, or transform variables.

Limitations of Descriptive Statistics:

1. **Simplification:** Descriptive statistics provide a simplified summary of data, which may not capture all of its complexity.

2. **Assumption of Normality:** Some statistics, like the mean and standard deviation, assume that the data is normally distributed, which may not always be the case.
3. **Influence of Outliers:** Extreme values can significantly affect measures like the mean and standard deviation, potentially leading to misinterpretations.

Descriptive statistics serve as the foundation of data analysis, helping data scientists uncover initial insights, detect anomalies, and make informed decisions about subsequent analyses. They provide a vital starting point for more advanced statistical techniques and modeling in the data science workflow.

3.4 Dealing with Missing Data

Missing data is a common issue encountered in datasets, and it's essential for data scientists to address it effectively during exploratory data analysis (EDA) and subsequent modeling. Missing data can arise due to various reasons, including data collection errors, survey non-responses, or sensor failures. Failing to handle missing data appropriately can lead to biased or erroneous results in data analysis.

Why Addressing Missing Data Matters:

1. **Accurate Analysis:** Missing data can distort statistical analyses, leading to inaccurate or biased results. Handling it correctly is crucial for obtaining valid insights.
2. **Data Quality:** Ensuring data quality is a fundamental aspect of any data science project. Dealing with missing data is part of maintaining data integrity.
3. **Preserving Sample Size:** Ignoring missing data can lead to a significant reduction in sample size, potentially reducing the statistical power of your analysis. Proper handling allows you to make the most of available data.

Methods for Handling Missing Data:

1. **Deletion:**
   o **Listwise Deletion:** Involves removing entire rows with missing values. While it's straightforward, it can result in a loss of valuable information.
   o **Pairwise Deletion:** Performs analysis on available data for each variable pair, allowing you to retain more observations for variables with less missing data.
2. **Imputation:**
   o **Mean/Median Imputation:** Replace missing values with the mean or median of the variable. It's simple but can distort the distribution.
   o **Mode Imputation:** For categorical data, replace missing values with the mode (most frequent category).
   o **Regression Imputation:** Predict missing values using regression models based on other variables.
   o **K-Nearest Neighbors (KNN) Imputation:** Replace missing values with the average of K-nearest data points based on similarity metrics.
   o **Multiple Imputation:** Generate multiple imputed datasets, analyze each, and then combine the results to account for uncertainty.
3. **Advanced Techniques:**
   o **Interpolation:** Use interpolation techniques to estimate missing values based on trends or patterns in the data.
   o **Time Series Methods:** For time series data, apply methods like forward filling or backward filling to impute missing values based on adjacent time points.
   o **Machine Learning Imputation:** Train machine learning models to predict missing values based on other features in the dataset.

Best Practices for Handling Missing Data:

1. **Understand the Missing Data Mechanism:** Determine whether the missing data is missing completely at random (MCAR), missing at random (MAR), or missing not at random (MNAR). This understanding can guide your choice of imputation method.

2. **Document the Process:** Keep a record of how missing data is handled, including the chosen imputation method. Transparency in your approach is critical for reproducibility.
3. **Sensitivity Analysis:** Perform sensitivity analyses to assess the impact of different imputation methods on your results. This helps gauge the robustness of your findings.
4. **Consider Data Collection Techniques:** If possible, address the root causes of missing data during data collection to reduce its occurrence in the first place.
5. **Consult Domain Experts:** Collaborate with domain experts to make informed decisions about handling missing data, especially when imputation methods involve assumptions.

Handling missing data is a nuanced and crucial step in the data analysis process. The choice of method should be guided by the nature of the data, the amount of missingness, and the impact on your research goals. Effective handling of missing data contributes to the reliability and validity of your data analysis and ensures that you can draw meaningful conclusions from your dataset.

CHAPTER 4: INTRODUCTION TO STATISTICS

4.1 Basic Statistical Concepts

Statistics is a discipline that provides the tools and techniques for making sense of data. Before diving into the more advanced aspects of statistics, it's essential to grasp some foundational concepts that serve as the building blocks for statistical analysis. In this section, we explore these basic statistical concepts.

1. Data Types:

- **Numerical Data:** Numerical data represents quantities and can be further categorized as:
  - **Continuous:** Data that can take any value within a range (e.g., height, weight).
  - **Discrete:** Data that can only take specific, separate values (e.g., number of children).
- **Categorical Data:** Categorical data represents categories or labels and includes nominal and ordinal data types.

2. Descriptive vs. Inferential Statistics:

- **Descriptive Statistics:** Descriptive statistics involve summarizing and describing data. Common descriptive measures include mean, median, mode, standard deviation, and quartiles.
- **Inferential Statistics:** Inferential statistics are used to make inferences or predictions about a population based on a sample of data. Techniques include hypothesis testing, confidence intervals, and regression analysis.

3. Population vs. Sample:

- **Population:** The entire group or set of individuals, items, or data under consideration in a study. It is often too large to study entirely.
- **Sample:** A subset of the population that is selected for analysis. The goal is for the sample to be representative of the population.

4. Variable:

- **Independent Variable:** The variable that is manipulated or controlled in experiments or analyses.
- **Dependent Variable:** The variable that is measured or observed in response to changes in the independent variable.

5. Statistical Distributions:

- **Normal Distribution:** A bell-shaped distribution characterized by its mean (μ) and standard deviation (σ). Many natural phenomena follow this distribution.
- **Binomial Distribution:** Models the number of successes in a fixed number of independent Bernoulli trials.
- **Poisson Distribution:** Models the number of events occurring in a fixed interval of time or space.

6. Central Limit Theorem:

- The Central Limit Theorem states that the sampling distribution of the sample mean approaches a normal distribution as the sample size increases, regardless of the shape of the population distribution.

7. Measures of Central Tendency:

- **Mean:** The arithmetic average of a set of values.
- **Median:** The middle value in a dataset when arranged in ascending or descending order.
- **Mode:** The value that occurs most frequently in a dataset.

8. Measures of Variability:

- **Range:** The difference between the maximum and minimum values in a dataset.
- **Variance:** A measure of how data points deviate from the mean. It quantifies the average squared difference between each data point and the mean.
- **Standard Deviation:** The square root of the variance. It provides a measure of the average distance between data points and the mean.

9. Percentiles:

- Percentiles are values that divide a dataset into 100 equal parts. For example, the 25th percentile is the value below which 25% of the data falls.

10. Correlation vs. Causation:

- **Correlation:** A statistical relationship between two variables. It does not imply causation, meaning that a correlation between two variables does not prove that one causes the other.
- **Causation:** A cause-and-effect relationship, where one variable directly influences or causes a change in another variable. Establishing causation requires more rigorous study designs, such as experiments.

4.2 Probability Distributions

Probability distributions are mathematical functions that describe the likelihood of various outcomes in a random experiment or data-generating process. Understanding these distributions is fundamental to many aspects of statistics and data science, as they provide insights into the behavior and characteristics of random variables.

Key Probability Distributions:

1. **Uniform Distribution:**
    o   **Description:** In a uniform distribution, all outcomes are equally likely. It's often depicted as a flat, rectangular shape.
    o   **Use Cases:** Modeling scenarios where each outcome is equally probable, such as rolling a fair six-sided die.
2. **Normal Distribution (Gaussian Distribution):**
    o   **Description:** The normal distribution is a bell-shaped, symmetric distribution characterized by its mean (μ) and standard deviation (σ). It's one of the most common distributions in nature.
    o   **Use Cases:** Modeling many natural phenomena, such as human height, exam scores, and measurement errors.
3. **Binomial Distribution:**
    o   **Description:** The binomial distribution models the number of successes (typically coded as 1) in a fixed number of independent Bernoulli trials (experiments with two possible outcomes: success or failure).
    o   **Use Cases:** Modeling scenarios like the number of heads obtained in multiple coin flips or the number of successful sales in a series of customer interactions.
4. **Poisson Distribution:**
    o   **Description:** The Poisson distribution models the number of events occurring in a fixed interval of time or space. It's often used for rare events with a known average rate.
    o   **Use Cases:** Modeling rare events such as the number of customer arrivals at a store, the number of accidents at an intersection, or the number of emails received per hour.
5. **Exponential Distribution:**

- o **Description:** The exponential distribution describes the time between events in a Poisson process, where events occur continuously and independently at a constant rate.
- o **Use Cases:** Modeling waiting times, such as the time between customer arrivals at a service center.

6. **Bernoulli Distribution:**
   - o **Description:** The Bernoulli distribution represents a single trial with two possible outcomes: success (usually coded as 1) or failure (usually coded as 0).
   - o **Use Cases:** Modeling binary events, like the success or failure of a single coin flip or the acceptance or rejection of a loan application.

7. **Geometric Distribution:**
   - o **Description:** The geometric distribution models the number of trials needed until the first success occurs in a sequence of independent Bernoulli trials.
   - o **Use Cases:** Modeling scenarios like the number of attempts required to make the first successful free throw in basketball.

Applications of Probability Distributions:

- **Hypothesis Testing:** Probability distributions are essential for conducting hypothesis tests, where you compare observed data to expected outcomes under certain assumptions.
- **Statistical Inference:** Distributions play a crucial role in estimating parameters and constructing confidence intervals.
- **Simulation:** Probability distributions are used in Monte Carlo simulations to model and analyze complex systems and processes.
- **Risk Assessment:** In finance and insurance, probability distributions are employed to assess and manage risk.
- **Machine Learning:** Distributions are used in machine learning algorithms, especially in generative models like Gaussian Naive Bayes and generative adversarial networks (GANs).

Understanding probability distributions allows data scientists to model and analyze real-world phenomena, make predictions, and draw conclusions based on data. Different situations may require different distributions, so having a working knowledge of various distributions is essential for sound statistical analysis and data-driven decision-making.

4.3 Hypothesis Testing

Hypothesis testing is a fundamental statistical technique used to make decisions and draw conclusions about populations based on sample data. It provides a structured framework for assessing whether observed differences or effects are statistically significant or if they could have occurred by random chance. Hypothesis testing is a cornerstone of scientific research, data analysis, and data-driven decision-making.

Key Components of Hypothesis Testing:

1. **Null Hypothesis (H0):** The null hypothesis is a statement of no effect or no difference. It represents the status quo or the assumption that there is no real effect or relationship in the population.
2. **Alternative Hypothesis (H1 or Ha):** The alternative hypothesis is the statement that contradicts the null hypothesis. It represents the researcher's claim or the assertion that there is a real effect or relationship in the population.
3. **Test Statistic:** The test statistic is a numerical value calculated from the sample data that measures the extent to which the sample evidence supports the alternative hypothesis.
4. **Significance Level (α):** The significance level, often denoted as α (alpha), is the predetermined threshold that defines the level of significance. Common values include 0.05 and 0.01, indicating a 5% or 1% chance of making a Type I error (rejecting the null hypothesis when it's true).
5. **P-value:** The p-value is the probability of observing a test statistic as extreme as, or more extreme than, the one calculated from the sample data, assuming the null hypothesis is true. A smaller p-value suggests stronger evidence against the null hypothesis.

Steps in Hypothesis Testing:

1. **Formulate Hypotheses:** Define the null and alternative hypotheses based on the research question or problem.
2. **Collect Data:** Gather relevant data through sampling or experiments.
3. **Choose a Test Statistic:** Select an appropriate statistical test based on the type of data and research question (e.g., t-test, chi-squared test, ANOVA).
4. **Set the Significance Level:** Decide on the significance level (α) to determine the threshold for statistical significance.
5. **Calculate the Test Statistic:** Compute the test statistic using the sample data and the chosen statistical test.
6. **Determine the P-value:** Find the p-value associated with the test statistic. A smaller p-value indicates stronger evidence against the null hypothesis.
7. **Make a Decision:** Compare the p-value to the significance level. If the p-value is less than or equal to α, reject the null hypothesis in favor of the alternative hypothesis; otherwise, fail to reject the null hypothesis.
8. **Draw Conclusions:** Interpret the results in the context of the research question. Conclusions may include statements like "there is sufficient evidence to suggest that..." or "there is not enough evidence to conclude that..."

Types of Errors in Hypothesis Testing:

- **Type I Error (False Positive):** Occurs when the null hypothesis is incorrectly rejected when it is actually true. This is a false alarm or a "false positive."
- **Type II Error (False Negative):** Occurs when the null hypothesis is incorrectly retained when it is actually false. This is a missed opportunity or a "false negative."

Common Applications of Hypothesis Testing:

- **Medical Research:** Testing the effectiveness of new drugs or treatments.
- **Quality Control:** Assessing the quality of manufactured products.

- **Market Research:** Investigating consumer preferences and behaviors.
- **A/B Testing:** Comparing the performance of different versions of a website or application.

Hypothesis testing is a powerful tool for making evidence-based decisions and drawing conclusions from data. It allows researchers and data scientists to rigorously assess the significance of their findings and provides a systematic approach to testing research hypotheses. Understanding hypothesis testing is essential for conducting reliable and credible statistical analyses.

4.4 Statistical Inference

Statistical inference is the process of drawing conclusions, making predictions, or estimating parameters about a population based on sample data. It extends the insights gained from hypothesis testing and provides a broader framework for making informed decisions and inferences in data science and research.

Key Concepts in Statistical Inference:

1. **Population and Sample:**
   - **Population:** The entire group or set of individuals, items, or data under consideration in a study. It is often too large to study entirely.
   - **Sample:** A subset of the population that is selected for analysis. The goal is for the sample to be representative of the population.
2. **Parameter and Statistic:**
   - **Parameter:** A numerical value that describes a characteristic of a population. Common parameters include population mean (μ) and population standard deviation (σ).
   - **Statistic:** A numerical value that summarizes a characteristic of a sample. Common statistics include sample mean (x) and sample standard deviation (s).
3. **Point Estimation:**

o **Point Estimate:** A single value that is used to estimate a population parameter. For example, using the sample mean to estimate the population mean.

4. **Confidence Interval:**
   o **Confidence Interval (CI):** A range of values that is likely to contain the true population parameter with a specified level of confidence (e.g., 95% confidence interval).
   o **Margin of Error:** The range added and subtracted from the point estimate to create the confidence interval.

5. **Hypothesis Testing and Inference:**
   o Hypothesis testing is a form of statistical inference used to make decisions about population parameters based on sample data. The process involves formulating null and alternative hypotheses and comparing them using statistical tests.

6. **Sampling Distributions:**
   o **Sampling Distribution:** A probability distribution of a statistic (e.g., sample mean) calculated from multiple samples of the same size from a population. The Central Limit Theorem often applies, making many sampling distributions approximately normal.

Methods of Statistical Inference:

1. **Confidence Intervals:**
   o Confidence intervals provide a range of plausible values for a population parameter. They are calculated using sample statistics and take into account variability in the data.

2. **Hypothesis Testing:**
   o Hypothesis testing helps assess the significance of observed effects or differences. It involves setting up null and alternative hypotheses, calculating test statistics, and comparing them to critical values or p-values.

3. **Regression Analysis:**
   o Regression analysis is used to estimate the relationship between one or more independent variables and a dependent variable. It allows for predictions and

inferences about how changes in independent variables affect the dependent variable.

4. **Bootstrapping:**
   o Bootstrapping is a resampling technique used to estimate the sampling distribution of a statistic by repeatedly drawing random samples with replacement from the observed data.

5. **Bayesian Inference:**
   o Bayesian inference is a probabilistic framework for making inferences based on prior knowledge and observed data. It provides posterior probability distributions for parameters of interest.

Applications of Statistical Inference:

- **Economics:** Estimating unemployment rates, inflation, and GDP growth.
- **Medical Research:** Assessing the effectiveness of treatments and interventions.
- **Market Research:** Predicting consumer behavior and market trends.
- **Environmental Science:** Estimating pollution levels and climate change impacts.
- **Quality Control:** Ensuring product quality and consistency.

Statistical inference is a powerful tool that enables data scientists and researchers to make informed decisions and draw meaningful conclusions from data. It plays a crucial role in hypothesis testing, parameter estimation, and prediction, providing a rigorous foundation for evidence-based decision-making in various fields.

CHAPTER 5: DATA WRANGLING

5.1 Data Transformation

Data transformation is a critical step in the data wrangling process. It involves altering the format, structure, or values of data to make it suitable for analysis, modeling, or visualization. Effective data transformation can help uncover hidden patterns, reduce noise, and ensure that data aligns with the specific requirements of a data science project.

Key Aspects of Data Transformation:

1. **Handling Missing Data:**
   o **Imputation:** Replacing missing values with estimated or calculated values based on the available data. Common imputation methods include mean, median, mode, or machine learning-based imputation.
   o **Deletion:** Removing rows or columns with missing data. This approach is suitable when missing data is negligible or when other data sources can fill the gaps.
2. **Data Encoding:**
   o **Categorical Encoding:** Converting categorical variables (non-numeric) into a numerical format. Common techniques include one-hot encoding, label encoding, and binary encoding.

- o **Ordinal Encoding:** Encoding ordinal categorical variables with meaningful numerical values that reflect their order or ranking.
3. **Scaling and Normalization:**
   - o **Feature Scaling:** Ensuring that variables are on a similar scale to prevent certain features from dominating in algorithms that rely on distance or magnitude, such as K-means clustering or gradient-based optimization.
   - o **Normalization:** Transforming data to have a common scale or distribution, often using techniques like Min-Max scaling or Z-score normalization.
4. **Log Transformation:**
   - o Applying a logarithmic transformation to data can be useful when dealing with highly skewed or exponentially distributed variables. This transformation can make data more symmetrical and suitable for statistical modeling.
5. **Data Aggregation:**
   - o Combining multiple data points into summary statistics, aggregating data at a higher level (e.g., calculating averages, sums, or counts), or generating new features from existing ones.
6. **Datetime Conversion:**
   - o Converting date and time data into a standardized format, extracting components like year, month, day, or hour, and creating time-based features.
7. **Binning and Discretization:**
   - o Grouping continuous numerical data into bins or intervals to simplify complex distributions and create categorical features.
8. **Handling Outliers:**
   - o Identifying and handling outliers through techniques like trimming, winsorizing, or transforming the data to be more robust to extreme values.
9. **Feature Engineering:**
   - o Creating new features that capture meaningful relationships or interactions between existing variables. This can involve mathematical operations, combining features, or domain-specific transformations.

Benefits of Data Transformation:

1. **Improved Model Performance:** Properly transformed data can lead to better-performing machine learning models, as it reduces noise and helps models capture underlying patterns.
2. **Easier Interpretation:** Transformed data often aligns more closely with the assumptions of statistical tests and models, making results easier to interpret.
3. **Efficient Storage and Processing:** Data transformation can lead to more efficient storage and faster computation, particularly when dealing with large datasets.
4. **Feature Selection:** Transformations can highlight which features are most relevant for modeling and analysis.

Challenges of Data Transformation:

1. **Information Loss:** Aggregating or encoding data can lead to information loss, potentially impacting the quality of analysis.
2. **Overfitting:** Aggressive feature engineering can lead to overfitting in machine learning models if not done judiciously.
3. **Complexity:** Complex transformations can be time-consuming and may require careful consideration of domain knowledge.

Data transformation is an art that balances the need to prepare data for analysis with the preservation of meaningful information. The choice of transformation techniques depends on the specific dataset, the goals of the analysis, and the requirements of the modeling process. When done effectively, data transformation sets the stage for insightful data analysis and robust machine learning models.

5.2 Feature Engineering

Feature engineering is the process of creating new features or modifying existing ones in a dataset to enhance its quality, improve the performance of machine learning models, and extract valuable information. It's a crucial step in data preparation and plays a pivotal role in the success of data science projects.

Key Concepts in Feature Engineering:

1. **Feature Creation:**
   o **Polynomial Features:** Creating new features by raising existing ones to a power. For instance, squaring a feature to capture quadratic relationships.
   o **Interaction Features:** Combining two or more existing features to capture interactions or synergistic effects that may influence the target variable.
   o **Domain-Specific Features:** Crafting features based on domain knowledge or specific insights into the problem. These features can be highly informative.
2. **Feature Transformation:**
   o **Logarithmic Transformation:** Applying a logarithmic function to a feature to address skewness and better represent exponential relationships.
   o **Box-Cox Transformation:** A family of power transformations that includes the logarithmic transformation as a special case. It can handle data with varying levels of skewness.
   o **Normalization and Standardization:** Scaling features to have specific means and variances to improve the performance of certain algorithms.
3. **Feature Extraction:**
   o **Principal Component Analysis (PCA):** A dimensionality reduction technique that transforms data into a new set of uncorrelated features (principal components) while retaining as much variance as possible.
   o **Feature Selection:** Identifying and keeping only the most relevant features while discarding redundant or irrelevant ones. Techniques include mutual information, feature importance from tree-based models, and recursive feature elimination.
4. **Handling Categorical Variables:**
   o **One-Hot Encoding:** Converting categorical variables into binary (0/1) columns for each category, enabling models to handle categorical data.

o **Target Encoding:** Encoding categorical variables based on the mean or other statistics of the target variable for each category.

5. **Time Series Features:**
   o **Lag Features:** Creating features based on previous time steps in time series data to capture temporal dependencies.
   o **Rolling Statistics:** Calculating rolling mean, median, or other statistics over a window of time to capture trends and seasonality.
6. **Text and Natural Language Processing (NLP) Features:**
   o **Tokenization:** Breaking text data into individual words or tokens for analysis.
   o **TF-IDF (Term Frequency-Inverse Document Frequency):** A numerical statistic that reflects the importance of a word in a document relative to a collection of documents. It's often used in text classification tasks.

Benefits of Feature Engineering:

1. **Improved Model Performance:** Well-engineered features can lead to better model accuracy, generalization, and robustness.
2. **Interpretability:** Feature engineering can make models more interpretable by creating features that align with domain knowledge.
3. **Dimensionality Reduction:** Feature engineering can help reduce the dimensionality of the dataset, making it more manageable and potentially improving model efficiency.
4. **Domain Knowledge Integration:** Domain experts can provide valuable insights that guide feature engineering, resulting in more meaningful and actionable features.

Challenges of Feature Engineering:

1. **Data Leakage:** Creating features that unintentionally incorporate information from the target variable can lead to data leakage and overfitting.
2. **Curse of Dimensionality:** Introducing too many features can lead to the curse of dimensionality, making the dataset harder to

work with and requiring more data to maintain model generalization.

3. **Complexity:** Feature engineering can be time-consuming and may require a deep understanding of the data and problem domain.

Feature engineering is both an art and a science, involving creativity, domain expertise, and technical skills. It's a dynamic and iterative process that often evolves as you gain a deeper understanding of the data and the problem at hand. Effective feature engineering can unlock the full potential of your data and significantly enhance the performance of your data science models.

5.3 Handling Categorical Data

Categorical data, which represents categories or labels rather than numerical values, is prevalent in many real-world datasets. Effectively handling categorical data is essential in data science, as it requires transformation into a format suitable for machine learning algorithms.

Types of Categorical Data:

1. **Nominal Data:** Categories without any inherent order or ranking. Examples include colors, countries, and animal species.
2. **Ordinal Data:** Categories with a meaningful order or ranking. Examples include education levels (e.g., high school, bachelor's, master's) or customer satisfaction ratings (e.g., "poor," "average," "excellent").

Techniques for Handling Categorical Data:

1. **One-Hot Encoding (Dummy Variables):**
   o **Description:** Converts each category into a binary column (0 or 1), creating a separate column for each category. Only one column will have a 1, indicating the presence of the category.

- o **Use Cases:** Nominal data with no inherent order. It is especially useful when categories have no meaningful numerical representation.
- o **Example:**

Color	Red	Blue	Green
Red	1	0	0
Blue	0	1	0
Green	0	0	1

2. **Label Encoding:**
   - o **Description:** Assigns a unique integer to each category. It is typically used for ordinal data, where the order matters.
   - o **Use Cases:** Ordinal data with a meaningful order or ranking.
   - o **Example:**

Education Level	Encoded
High School	0
Bachelor's	1
Master's	2

3. **Target Encoding (Mean Encoding):**
   - o **Description:** Replaces each category with the mean of the target variable for that category. It can be useful for nominal or ordinal data, especially in classification tasks.
   - o **Use Cases:** Any categorical data where the target variable differs by category.
   - o **Example:**

City	Target
New York	0.65
Boston	0.72
Chicago	0.61

4. **Frequency Encoding:**

- o **Description:** Replaces each category with the frequency or count of that category in the dataset.
- o **Use Cases:** Nominal data where the frequency of occurrence is relevant.
- o **Example:**

Animal Frequency
Dog   45
Cat   30
Rabbit 12

5. **Binary Encoding:**
   - o **Description:** Combines binary representations of integers to encode categories. It works well for nominal data with many categories.
   - o **Use Cases:** Nominal data with a large number of categories.
   - o **Example:** Suppose there are six categories (0 to 5):

Category Binary Encoding
0   000
1   001
2   010
3   011
4   100
5   101

Considerations for Handling Categorical Data:

1. **Choosing the Right Encoding Method:** The choice of encoding method depends on the type of categorical data, the problem at hand, and the specific machine learning algorithm you plan to use.
2. **Dealing with High Cardinality:** High cardinality (a large number of unique categories) can be challenging. In such cases, techniques like target encoding or binary encoding may be preferable to one-hot encoding.

3. **Feature Scaling:** Some machine learning algorithms may require feature scaling after encoding to ensure that categorical features do not dominate the model.
4. **Handling New Categories:** When new categories appear in the test data that were not seen during training, it's essential to have a strategy to handle them, such as assigning a default value or using a category catch-all.

Handling categorical data effectively is crucial for building accurate and reliable machine learning models. The choice of encoding method should align with the nature of the data and the goals of the analysis, ultimately improving the model's predictive performance.

5.4 Normalization and Scaling

Normalization and scaling are preprocessing techniques used to transform numerical features in a dataset to a consistent range or distribution. These techniques are crucial in data preprocessing and are often employed before applying machine learning algorithms. Normalization and scaling help in achieving better model performance, especially for algorithms that rely on distance measures or gradient descent optimization.

Normalization vs. Scaling:

- **Normalization** is the process of scaling a feature to have a range between 0 and 1. It's particularly useful when the features have different units or scales, and you want to bring them to a common scale.
- **Scaling** involves adjusting the range of features to be centered around a mean of 0 with a standard deviation of 1. This technique assumes that the data follows a roughly normal distribution.

Techniques for Normalization and Scaling:

1. **Min-Max Scaling (Normalization):**

- o **Description:** Scales the feature values to a specified range, usually [0, 1], by applying the following formula:

$$Xnormalized=(X-Xmin)/(Xmax-Xmin)Xn$$
$$ormalized=(X-Xmin)/(Xmax-Xmin)$$

- o **Use Cases:** When you want to preserve the relative relationships between feature values while ensuring they are within a specific range.

2. **Z-Score Normalization (Standardization):**
   - o **Description:** Transforms the feature values to have a mean (average) of 0 and a standard deviation of 1 by applying the following formula:

$$Xstandardized=(X-Xmean)/XstdXs$$
$$tandardized=(X-Xmean)/Xstd$$

- o **Use Cases:** Suitable when you assume that the data follows a normal distribution or when algorithms require features to be centered around zero.

3. **Robust Scaling:**
   - o **Description:** Scales the feature values by removing the median and scaling to the interquartile range (IQR) to make the transformation more robust to outliers.
   - o **Use Cases:** Effective when dealing with datasets containing outliers that can skew the mean and standard deviation.

4. **Log Transformation:**
   - o **Description:** Applies a logarithmic function to the feature values. This is particularly useful for reducing the impact of extreme values and handling highly skewed data.
   - o **Use Cases:** When the data exhibits a skewed distribution, such as income or population.

5. **Scaling to Unit Vector (Normalization):**
   - o **Description:** Scales the feature values to have a Euclidean norm (L2 norm) of 1. Each data point becomes a point on the unit circle in multidimensional space.
- o **Use Cases:** Useful when you want to preserve the direction of data points while ensuring they have a consistent length.

Considerations for Normalization and Scaling:

1. **Impact on Algorithms:** The choice of normalization or scaling method can significantly affect the performance of machine learning algorithms. Some algorithms, like k-means clustering or principal component analysis (PCA), are sensitive to feature scaling.
2. **Outlier Handling:** Be cautious when applying normalization or scaling to datasets with outliers. Robust scaling or log transformation can be more appropriate in such cases.
3. **Normalization Order:** The order in which you normalize or scale features can matter. In some cases, it may be necessary to normalize or scale all features simultaneously to avoid introducing bias.
4. **Validation Data:** When using normalization or scaling, it's crucial to apply the same transformation to both the training and validation/test datasets to ensure consistent preprocessing.
5. **Domain Knowledge:** Consider the nature of the data and domain-specific insights when choosing a normalization or scaling technique. Different datasets may benefit from different methods.

Normalization and scaling are essential preprocessing steps that help ensure that features contribute to machine learning models in a meaningful way. The choice of technique depends on the characteristics of the data and the requirements of the machine learning algorithm being used, so it's important to select the method that best suits the specific problem at hand.

CHAPTER 6: MACHINE LEARNING BASICS

6.1 What is Machine Learning?

Machine learning is a subset of artificial intelligence (AI) that focuses on the development of algorithms and statistical models that enable computer systems to learn and make predictions or decisions without being explicitly programmed. In essence, machine learning empowers computers to analyze data, recognize patterns, and improve their performance through experience.

Key Characteristics of Machine Learning:

1. **Learning from Data:** Machine learning algorithms learn from data. They use historical or training data to identify patterns, relationships, and trends that can inform future decisions.
2. **Generalization:** Machine learning models generalize from the data they have seen to make predictions or decisions about new, unseen data. This ability to generalize is a fundamental aspect of machine learning.
3. **Adaptation:** Machine learning models adapt and improve their performance as they encounter more data. They can refine their predictions or behavior over time.

Types of Machine Learning:

1. **Supervised Learning:** In supervised learning, algorithms learn from labeled examples. They are provided with input-output pairs (features and corresponding labels) and learn to map inputs to outputs. Common tasks include classification (assigning labels to inputs) and regression (predicting continuous values).
2. **Unsupervised Learning:** Unsupervised learning involves algorithms learning from unlabeled data to discover patterns or structures within the data. Common tasks include clustering (grouping similar data points) and dimensionality reduction (reducing the number of features while preserving information).
3. **Semi-Supervised Learning:** Semi-supervised learning combines elements of both supervised and unsupervised learning. Algorithms are trained on a combination of labeled and unlabeled data.
4. **Reinforcement Learning:** In reinforcement learning, algorithms learn by interacting with an environment. They receive feedback in the form of rewards or penalties based on their actions and make decisions to maximize cumulative rewards. This approach is often used in tasks like game playing and autonomous control.

Machine Learning in Practice:

Machine learning has found applications across various domains, including:

- **Natural Language Processing (NLP):** Powering chatbots, language translation, sentiment analysis, and text generation.
- **Computer Vision:** Enabling facial recognition, object detection, image and video analysis, and autonomous driving.
- **Healthcare:** Assisting in disease diagnosis, medical image analysis, and drug discovery.
- **Finance:** Supporting fraud detection, risk assessment, algorithmic trading, and credit scoring.
- **Recommendation Systems:** Personalizing content recommendations in e-commerce, streaming services, and advertising.

The Machine Learning Process:

1. **Data Collection:** Gathering and preparing relevant data is the first step in a machine learning project.
2. **Data Preprocessing:** Cleaning, transforming, and encoding data to make it suitable for modeling.
3. **Feature Engineering:** Creating or selecting the most relevant features (input variables) for the task.
4. **Model Selection:** Choosing an appropriate machine learning algorithm based on the problem type and dataset.
5. **Training:** Feeding the model with labeled data to learn patterns and relationships.
6. **Evaluation:** Assessing the model's performance using metrics and validation techniques.
7. **Hyperparameter Tuning:** Fine-tuning model settings to optimize performance.
8. **Deployment:** Integrating the trained model into a real-world application.
9. **Monitoring and Maintenance:** Continuously monitoring model performance and updating as needed.

Machine learning has evolved rapidly and is becoming increasingly accessible with the availability of open-source libraries and tools. It has the potential to revolutionize industries and drive innovation across diverse domains, making it a fascinating and dynamic field to explore and apply in practice.

6.2 Types of Machine Learning

Machine learning encompasses a variety of approaches, each tailored to different types of tasks and data. Understanding these types is essential for choosing the right algorithm and approach for a given problem. Here are the primary types of machine learning:

1. Supervised Learning:

- **Definition:** In supervised learning, the algorithm is trained on a labeled dataset, where each data point consists of both input features and the corresponding target or output variable. The goal is to learn a mapping from inputs to outputs.

- **Common Tasks:**
  - o **Classification:** Assigning data points to predefined categories or labels. Examples include spam email detection, image classification, and sentiment analysis.
  - o **Regression:** Predicting a continuous numerical value. Examples include house price prediction, stock price forecasting, and temperature prediction.
- **Examples of Algorithms:** Linear Regression, Decision Trees, Support Vector Machines, Neural Networks, Naive Bayes, k-Nearest Neighbors (k-NN).

2. Unsupervised Learning:

- **Definition:** Unsupervised learning involves training on an unlabeled dataset, and the algorithm's objective is to find patterns, structures, or relationships within the data without guidance from target labels.
- **Common Tasks:**
  - o **Clustering:** Grouping similar data points together based on their characteristics. Examples include customer segmentation and image clustering.
  - o **Dimensionality Reduction:** Reducing the number of features while preserving the most important information. Examples include Principal Component Analysis (PCA) and t-distributed Stochastic Neighbor Embedding (t-SNE).
- **Examples of Algorithms:** K-Means Clustering, Hierarchical Clustering, Principal Component Analysis (PCA), Independent Component Analysis (ICA), Autoencoders.

3. Semi-Supervised Learning:

- **Definition:** Semi-supervised learning combines elements of both supervised and unsupervised learning. It uses a combination of labeled and unlabeled data for training. This approach is useful when acquiring labeled data is costly or time-consuming.
- **Use Cases:** Text classification with a limited labeled dataset, where the model leverages a large pool of unlabeled text data.

4. Reinforcement Learning:

- **Definition:** Reinforcement learning is concerned with training agents to make sequences of decisions or take actions in an environment to maximize cumulative rewards. The agent learns from trial and error, adjusting its actions based on feedback.
- **Components:**
  - **Agent:** The learner or decision-maker.
  - **Environment:** The external system with which the agent interacts.
  - **Actions:** The choices or decisions made by the agent.
  - **Rewards:** The feedback or outcomes provided by the environment.
- **Use Cases:** Game playing (e.g., AlphaGo), robotics, autonomous driving, recommendation systems, and financial trading.
- **Examples of Algorithms:** Q-Learning, Deep Q-Networks (DQN), Proximal Policy Optimization (PPO), and Actor-Critic methods.

5. Self-Supervised Learning:

- **Definition:** Self-supervised learning is a type of unsupervised learning where the algorithm generates its own labels from the data. It often involves solving pretext tasks to create labeled data, which can then be used for downstream tasks.
- **Use Cases:** Pretraining neural networks for various tasks, such as natural language understanding or computer vision.

These types of machine learning are not mutually exclusive, and hybrid approaches can be employed to solve complex problems. The choice of which type to use depends on the nature of the data, the task at hand, and the available resources. Machine learning continues to evolve, with researchers developing new techniques and models that push the boundaries of what's possible in various domains.

6.3 Supervised Learning

Supervised learning is one of the fundamental branches of machine learning, where algorithms learn to make predictions or decisions by training on a labeled dataset. In supervised learning, each data point in the training dataset consists of both input features and corresponding target values or labels. The primary goal is to learn a mapping from inputs to outputs, enabling the algorithm to make predictions on new, unseen data.

Key Characteristics of Supervised Learning:

1. **Labeled Data:** Supervised learning relies on labeled training data, where each example has known target values or labels. These labels serve as the ground truth for the learning process.
2. **Prediction or Classification:** Supervised learning tasks fall into two main categories:
   o **Regression:** When the target variable is a continuous numerical value, and the goal is to predict or estimate this value. Examples include predicting house prices, stock prices, or temperature.
   o **Classification:** When the target variable consists of discrete categories or labels, and the goal is to assign each input data point to one of these categories. Examples include spam detection, image classification, and sentiment analysis.
3. **Model Training:** During the training phase, the algorithm uses the labeled data to learn patterns, relationships, or decision boundaries that map inputs to outputs.
4. **Model Evaluation:** The model's performance is assessed using metrics appropriate for the task, such as Mean Squared Error (MSE) for regression or accuracy, precision, recall, and F1-score for classification.
5. **Generalization:** Once trained, the model can make predictions or classifications on new, previously unseen data, allowing it to generalize from the training data to new examples.

Common Supervised Learning Algorithms:

1. **Linear Regression:** Used for regression tasks, linear regression models the relationship between input features and a continuous target variable by fitting a linear equation to the data.
2. **Logistic Regression:** Despite its name, logistic regression is used for binary classification tasks. It models the probability that an input belongs to one of two classes.
3. **Decision Trees:** Decision trees are versatile and can be used for both regression and classification tasks. They create a tree-like structure of decisions based on feature values to make predictions.
4. **Random Forest:** An ensemble learning method that combines multiple decision trees to improve predictive accuracy and reduce overfitting.
5. **Support Vector Machines (SVM):** Used for classification tasks, SVMs find the optimal hyperplane that best separates data into different classes.
6. **Neural Networks:** Deep neural networks, including convolutional neural networks (CNNs) for image data and recurrent neural networks (RNNs) for sequential data, are powerful models used for various supervised learning tasks.
7. **k-Nearest Neighbors (k-NN):** k-NN is used for both regression and classification. It makes predictions based on the majority class or the average of k-nearest data points in the training dataset.

Applications of Supervised Learning:

Supervised learning has a wide range of applications in various domains, including:

- **Healthcare:** Predicting disease diagnosis and patient outcomes.
- **Finance:** Credit scoring, fraud detection, and stock price prediction.
- **Natural Language Processing (NLP):** Language translation, sentiment analysis, and chatbots.

- **Computer Vision:** Object detection, image segmentation, and facial recognition.
- **Recommendation Systems:** Personalized content recommendations in e-commerce and streaming platforms.

Supervised learning is a foundational concept in machine learning and serves as the basis for many advanced techniques and models. It continues to play a pivotal role in solving real-world problems by making data-driven predictions and decisions.

6.4 Unsupervised Learning

Unsupervised learning is a branch of machine learning where algorithms are trained on datasets that lack labeled target values or outputs. Instead, the goal of unsupervised learning is to discover patterns, structures, or relationships within the data without any explicit guidance. This makes it particularly useful for tasks where the objective is to explore and understand the data's inherent characteristics.

Key Characteristics of Unsupervised Learning:

1. **Unlabeled Data:** In unsupervised learning, the training dataset consists of raw data without associated target labels. This data may include a set of input features, but there are no predefined output values.
2. **Exploratory Nature:** Unsupervised learning is often exploratory in nature, allowing algorithms to uncover hidden structures or insights within the data that may not be apparent through manual inspection.
3. **Common Tasks:** Unsupervised learning tasks can be broadly categorized into two main types:
   o **Clustering:** The goal is to group similar data points together into clusters or categories based on shared characteristics. Clustering helps identify patterns and structure within data.
   o **Dimensionality Reduction:** The aim is to reduce the number of features or variables in the data while retaining essential

information. This is valuable for simplifying complex datasets and improving model efficiency.

Common Unsupervised Learning Algorithms:

1. **K-Means Clustering:** A popular clustering algorithm that partitions data into k clusters based on similarity. It assigns data points to the nearest cluster center, known as a centroid.
2. **Hierarchical Clustering:** This approach builds a hierarchy of clusters by successively merging or splitting groups of data points based on similarity.
3. **Principal Component Analysis (PCA):** A dimensionality reduction technique that transforms high-dimensional data into a lower-dimensional representation while preserving the most important information.
4. **Independent Component Analysis (ICA):** A method that separates a multivariate signal into additive, independent components.
5. **Autoencoders:** Neural network models that learn to encode and decode data, effectively reducing dimensionality and learning compact representations.

Applications of Unsupervised Learning:

Unsupervised learning is applied in a variety of domains for tasks such as:

- **Customer Segmentation:** Grouping customers based on purchasing behavior for targeted marketing.
- **Anomaly Detection:** Identifying rare or unusual patterns in data, such as fraudulent transactions or network intrusions.
- **Topic Modeling:** Extracting underlying themes or topics from large text corpora.
- **Image Compression:** Reducing the storage size of images while retaining visual quality.
- **Feature Engineering:** Creating new features or variables for supervised learning tasks.

Unsupervised learning can also serve as a preprocessing step for supervised learning by reducing dimensionality or identifying relevant features. It plays a crucial role in data exploration and pattern discovery, helping uncover valuable insights and knowledge from unstructured or unlabeled data.

6.5 Evaluation Metrics

Evaluation metrics are essential tools in machine learning for assessing the performance of models and algorithms. These metrics help data scientists and machine learning practitioners quantitatively measure how well a model is performing on a given task. The choice of evaluation metric depends on the specific problem and the type of machine learning task (e.g., classification, regression) being addressed.

Here are some commonly used evaluation metrics:

1. Classification Metrics:

In classification tasks, where the goal is to assign data points to predefined categories or labels, several metrics can help gauge a model's performance:

- **Accuracy:** Accuracy measures the ratio of correctly predicted instances to the total number of instances in the dataset. It's suitable for balanced datasets but may not be appropriate when classes are imbalanced.
- **Precision:** Precision calculates the ratio of correctly predicted positive instances (true positives) to the total number of positive predictions (true positives + false positives). It indicates how well the model avoids false positive errors.
- **Recall (Sensitivity or True Positive Rate):** Recall calculates the ratio of correctly predicted positive instances (true positives) to the total number of actual positive instances (true positives + false negatives). It quantifies how well the model captures positive instances.
- **F1-Score:** The F1-score is the harmonic mean of precision and recall. It balances precision and recall and is particularly useful when there is an imbalance between the classes.

- **Area Under the Receiver Operating Characteristic Curve (AUC-ROC):** ROC curves are used for binary classification. AUC-ROC quantifies the model's ability to distinguish between classes across different threshold values.
- **Area Under the Precision-Recall Curve (AUC-PR):** Similar to AUC-ROC, AUC-PR evaluates the model's performance across different thresholds, focusing on precision and recall.

2. Regression Metrics:

In regression tasks, where the goal is to predict numerical values, different metrics are used to assess the model's predictive accuracy:

- **Mean Absolute Error (MAE):** MAE calculates the average absolute difference between predicted and actual values. It is less sensitive to outliers.
- **Mean Squared Error (MSE):** MSE calculates the average of squared differences between predicted and actual values. It gives more weight to large errors.
- **Root Mean Squared Error (RMSE):** RMSE is the square root of MSE and provides a measure of the typical error size in the predictions. It's in the same units as the target variable.
- **R-squared (R2):** R2 measures the proportion of the variance in the target variable that is explained by the model. It ranges from 0 to 1, with higher values indicating a better fit.

3. Clustering Metrics:

For unsupervised learning tasks like clustering, where the goal is to group similar data points together, metrics can assess the quality of clusters:

- **Silhouette Score:** The silhouette score measures how similar each data point in one cluster is to the data points in the same cluster compared to the nearest neighboring cluster. It ranges from -1 to 1, with higher values indicating better-defined clusters.
- **Davies-Bouldin Index:** This index quantifies the average similarity between each cluster and its most similar cluster, with lower values indicating better clustering.

- **Adjusted Rand Index (ARI):** ARI measures the similarity between true labels and predicted clusters, adjusting for chance. It ranges from -1 to 1, with higher values indicating better clustering.

4. Time Series Metrics:

For time series forecasting tasks, specific metrics are used to assess the accuracy of predictions over time:

- **Mean Absolute Percentage Error (MAPE):** MAPE calculates the percentage difference between predicted and actual values, providing a measure of prediction accuracy.
- **Root Mean Squared Error (RMSE):** RMSE, as mentioned earlier, is commonly used to measure the error in time series forecasting.
- **Mean Absolute Error (MAE):** MAE can also be applied to time series data to measure the average absolute difference between predicted and actual values.
- **Lag Plot:** A visual diagnostic tool to assess the randomness or autocorrelation of time series data.

The choice of evaluation metric depends on the problem's context and the trade-offs between precision and recall, bias and variance, or other relevant factors. Careful consideration of the appropriate metric is essential to ensure that the model's performance is accurately assessed and aligns with the problem's goals.

CHAPTER 8: CLUSTERING AND DIMENSIONALITY REDUCTION

8.1 K-Means Clustering

K-Means clustering is a popular unsupervised machine learning algorithm that helps us group similar data points into clusters or categories based on their inherent characteristics. It's a fundamental technique for exploring patterns and structure within data when we don't have predefined labels.

How K-Means Clustering Works:

K-Means operates on the principle of partitioning data points into K clusters, where K is a user-defined hyperparameter. The algorithm follows these steps:

1. **Initialization:** Randomly select K initial cluster centroids, where each centroid represents the center of a potential cluster.
2. **Assignment:** Assign each data point to the nearest centroid based on a distance metric, often using Euclidean distance.
3. **Update:** Recalculate the centroids of the clusters by taking the mean of all data points assigned to each cluster.
4. **Iteration:** Repeat the assignment and update steps until convergence. Convergence typically occurs when the centroids

no longer change significantly or after a fixed number of iterations.

Key Characteristics of K-Means:

- **Hard Clustering:** K-Means assigns each data point to a single cluster, known as hard clustering. This means that a data point belongs exclusively to the cluster whose centroid it is closest to.
- **Centroid-Based:** Clusters are defined by their centroids, which are the mean of all data points within the cluster. Centroids are representative of the cluster's characteristics.
- **Sensitivity to Initialization:** K-Means can be sensitive to the initial placement of centroids, which can lead to different clustering results. To mitigate this, the algorithm is often run multiple times with different initializations, and the best result is chosen.

Applications of K-Means Clustering:

K-Means clustering finds applications in a wide range of fields, including:

1. **Customer Segmentation:** Grouping customers based on purchasing behavior for targeted marketing.
2. **Image Compression:** Reducing the storage size of images by representing similar pixel values with a single value.
3. **Anomaly Detection:** Identifying unusual patterns or outliers in data.
4. **Document Clustering:** Grouping similar documents together for topic modeling or search engines.
5. **Recommendation Systems:** Clustering users or products for personalized recommendations.

Challenges and Considerations:

K-Means has some limitations and considerations:

- **Number of Clusters (K):** Choosing the right number of clusters (K) can be challenging. Various methods, such as the elbow method or silhouette analysis, can help determine an optimal K value.

- **Sensitive to Outliers:** K-Means is sensitive to outliers, which can disproportionately influence cluster centroids.
- **Scaling:** Data scaling is essential to ensure that features with different units or scales do not dominate the clustering process.
- **Non-Convex Shapes:** K-Means assumes that clusters are spherical and equally sized, which may not always be the case. For non-convex clusters, other clustering algorithms like DBSCAN may be more appropriate.

8.2 Hierarchical Clustering

Hierarchical clustering is an unsupervised machine learning technique used to build a hierarchy of clusters within a dataset. Unlike K-Means clustering, which requires the user to specify the number of clusters (K) beforehand, hierarchical clustering creates a tree-like structure of clusters, or a dendrogram, which can be further analyzed to determine the desired number of clusters. Hierarchical clustering is flexible and widely used in various fields, including biology, finance, and social sciences.

How Hierarchical Clustering Works:

Hierarchical clustering can be divided into two main approaches: agglomerative (bottom-up) and divisive (top-down). The agglomerative approach is more common and is described here:

1. **Initialization:** Start by treating each data point as a single cluster. If there are N data points, you initially have N clusters, each containing one data point.
2. **Agglomeration:** Repeatedly merge the two closest clusters into a single cluster until only one cluster remains. The distance between clusters is measured using a linkage method, such as single linkage (minimum pairwise distance), complete linkage (maximum pairwise distance), or average linkage (average pairwise distance).
3. **Dendrogram Creation:** As clusters are merged, a dendrogram is constructed. The dendrogram visually represents the hierarchy of

clusters, with each branch representing the merging of clusters at a specific distance threshold.

4. **Cluster Selection:** To determine the number of clusters, you can cut the dendrogram at a desired height, creating a specific number of clusters. Alternatively, you can choose the number of clusters based on the application and domain knowledge.

Key Characteristics of Hierarchical Clustering:

- **Hierarchical Structure:** Hierarchical clustering creates a tree-like structure of clusters, allowing for a flexible exploration of different levels of granularity in the data.
- **No Need to Specify K:** Unlike K-Means, hierarchical clustering does not require you to specify the number of clusters beforehand, making it suitable for exploratory data analysis.
- **Interpretability:** The dendrogram provides an interpretable visualization of cluster relationships, showing how clusters are nested and related to each other.

Applications of Hierarchical Clustering:

Hierarchical clustering has various applications, including:

1. **Biology:** Grouping genes with similar expression patterns for gene expression analysis.
2. **Customer Segmentation:** Creating customer segments based on purchasing behavior or demographics.
3. **Image Analysis:** Clustering images with similar content or style for content-based image retrieval.
4. **Taxonomy and Classification:** Building hierarchical taxonomies for organizing and classifying data.
5. **Anomaly Detection:** Identifying unusual patterns or outliers in data.

Challenges and Considerations:

- **Scalability:** Hierarchical clustering can be computationally expensive for large datasets, as it requires computing pairwise distances between data points.

- **Choice of Linkage Method:** The choice of linkage method can affect the clustering result, so it's essential to consider which method aligns with the data's characteristics.
- **Interpretation:** Interpreting the dendrogram and choosing the right number of clusters can be subjective and dependent on domain knowledge.

8.3 Principal Component Analysis (PCA)

Principal Component Analysis (PCA) is a widely used dimensionality reduction technique in machine learning and data analysis. PCA aims to transform high-dimensional data into a lower-dimensional space while retaining as much of the original information as possible. It achieves this by identifying the principal components, which are new orthogonal axes in the data space that capture the most significant variance.

How PCA Works:

1. **Data Standardization:** Start by standardizing the data, ensuring that each feature has a mean of 0 and a standard deviation of 1. Standardization is important as it gives equal weight to all features, preventing some features from dominating the analysis.
2. **Covariance Matrix Calculation:** Compute the covariance matrix of the standardized data. The covariance matrix measures how features vary together. Off-diagonal elements represent the covariances between pairs of features, while diagonal elements represent variances.
3. **Eigenvalue Decomposition:** Perform eigenvalue decomposition on the covariance matrix. This decomposition yields eigenvectors and eigenvalues. The eigenvectors are the principal components, and the eigenvalues indicate the amount of variance explained by each principal component.
4. **Sorting Principal Components:** Sort the eigenvectors in descending order of their corresponding eigenvalues. The principal components are ordered by the amount of variance they capture, with the first principal component explaining the most variance.

5. **Dimensionality Reduction:** Select a subset of the principal components based on the desired dimensionality reduction. Retaining the top K principal components (those with the highest eigenvalues) is a common choice, where K is the desired reduced dimensionality.
6. **Data Transformation:** Project the original data onto the selected principal components to obtain the lower-dimensional representation of the data.

Key Characteristics of PCA:

- **Dimensionality Reduction:** PCA reduces the dimensionality of data, which is beneficial for visualization, interpretation, and reducing the risk of overfitting in machine learning models.
- **Decorrelation:** Principal components are orthogonal (uncorrelated) with each other, meaning they do not contain redundant information.
- **Variance Maximization:** PCA aims to retain as much variance as possible in the lower-dimensional representation. The first principal component captures the most variance, followed by the second, and so on.

Applications of PCA:

PCA finds applications in various fields, including:

1. **Image Compression:** Reducing the size of image data while preserving essential information.
2. **Feature Selection:** Identifying the most important features in data by examining the contribution of each feature to the principal components.
3. **Exploratory Data Analysis:** Reducing high-dimensional data to visualize clusters, patterns, or trends more effectively.
4. **Noise Reduction:** Removing noise from data by projecting it onto the principal components that capture the signal.

Challenges and Considerations:

- **Loss of Interpretability:** The interpretability of principal components decreases as the dimensionality of the data is reduced.
- **Choice of Dimensionality:** Selecting the appropriate number of principal components or the reduced dimensionality is often a subjective decision.
- **Data Interpretation:** Understanding the meaning of the principal components can be challenging, especially when dealing with high-dimensional data.

8.4 t-SNE: t-Distributed Stochastic Neighbor Embedding

t-Distributed Stochastic Neighbor Embedding (t-SNE) is a popular dimensionality reduction and visualization technique used to map high-dimensional data into a lower-dimensional space. Unlike methods like Principal Component Analysis (PCA), t-SNE is particularly effective at preserving the local structure and revealing clusters or groups of data points. It is widely used in data analysis, machine learning, and data visualization.

How t-SNE Works:

1. **Similarity Measurement:** t-SNE starts by computing pairwise similarities or affinities between data points in the high-dimensional space. The choice of similarity metric can vary, but a common choice is Gaussian similarity based on Euclidean distances.
2. **Probability Distribution:** These pairwise similarities are converted into conditional probability distributions that indicate the likelihood of selecting one data point as a neighbor of another. The similarity values are transformed into probabilities using a Gaussian kernel.
3. **Low-Dimensional Mapping:** In parallel, t-SNE constructs a similar probability distribution in the lower-dimensional space, initially filled with random data points.
4. **Minimizing the Kullback-Leibler Divergence:** The main objective of t-SNE is to minimize the Kullback-Leibler (KL)

divergence between the two probability distributions: the one that encodes pairwise similarities in the high-dimensional space and the one in the low-dimensional space. This optimization aims to place similar data points close to each other in the low-dimensional representation while spreading dissimilar points apart.

5. **Gradient Descent:** Optimization techniques like gradient descent are used to iteratively adjust the positions of data points in the lower-dimensional space to minimize the KL divergence. The optimization process continues until convergence.

Key Characteristics of t-SNE:

- **Preserving Local Structure:** t-SNE excels at preserving the local relationships and clusters present in the high-dimensional data, making it particularly useful for visualizing data clusters and groups.
- **Non-Linearity:** Unlike PCA, t-SNE is inherently non-linear and can capture complex relationships among data points.
- **Random Initialization:** t-SNE often provides different results upon multiple runs due to the use of random initialization. Therefore, it is recommended to perform the algorithm multiple times and select the best result.

Applications of t-SNE:

t-SNE has a wide range of applications, including:

1. **Data Visualization:** Visualizing high-dimensional data to reveal clusters, patterns, or anomalies.
2. **Exploratory Data Analysis:** Gaining insights into complex datasets by projecting them into a lower-dimensional space.
3. **Feature Engineering:** Selecting relevant features and reducing dimensionality before training machine learning models.
4. **Natural Language Processing (NLP):** Visualizing word embeddings or document representations in NLP tasks.
5. **Biology:** Analyzing and visualizing gene expression data, protein-protein interactions, and more.

Challenges and Considerations:

- **Hyperparameters:** t-SNE has hyperparameters such as the perplexity value, which controls the balance between preserving global and local structures. The choice of perplexity can affect the results.
- **Computational Intensity:** t-SNE can be computationally intensive, especially for large datasets. Approximate methods like the Barnes-Hut t-SNE can be used to speed up computations.

CHAPTER 9: INTRODUCTION TO BIG DATA

9.1 What is Big Data?

In the digital age, the term "Big Data" has become ubiquitous, often used to describe the unprecedented volume of data generated by our increasingly interconnected world. Big Data is more than just a buzzword; it represents a transformative shift in the way we collect, store, process, and analyze information. To truly grasp the concept of Big Data, we need to explore the Four Vs—Volume, Velocity, Variety, and Veracity—that define it.

1. Volume: The Sheer Size

At the heart of Big Data is its sheer volume. It refers to the vast amount of data that is generated daily. This data can range from structured data (like databases and spreadsheets) to unstructured data (like text, images, and videos). The volume of Big Data is measured in petabytes, exabytes, and beyond.

For example, consider the data generated by social media platforms like Facebook and Twitter. Users generate millions of posts, comments, and images every minute, contributing to the staggering volume of data that these platforms manage.

2. Velocity: The Speed of Data Generation

Velocity refers to the speed at which data is generated and how quickly it needs to be processed and analyzed. With the advent of real-time data streams from sources like sensors, IoT devices, and social media, data is pouring in at an unprecedented pace.

For instance, financial trading platforms rely on sub-millisecond updates to make split-second decisions, while autonomous vehicles process sensor data in real-time to navigate safely.

3. Variety: The Diversity of Data Types

Variety encompasses the diverse types of data that fall under the Big Data umbrella. This includes structured data, unstructured data, and semi-structured data. Big Data encompasses text, images, audio, video, geospatial data, and more. Dealing with this variety often requires specialized tools and techniques.

Think about the data generated by a healthcare system: patient records, medical images, doctor's notes, and sensor data from wearables. All of these data types need to be integrated and analyzed for a comprehensive view of a patient's health.

4. Veracity: The Trustworthiness of Data

Veracity relates to the trustworthiness and quality of the data. In the world of Big Data, data can be messy, incomplete, or inaccurate. Veracity challenges arise from sources like user-generated content, sensor errors, and data integration issues. Ensuring data quality is a critical aspect of handling Big Data.

Consider the analysis of sentiment on social media. Sarcasm, slang, and misspellings can make it challenging to accurately determine sentiment from text data, highlighting veracity concerns.

The Fifth V: Value

While not always included in the Four Vs, "Value" is a crucial aspect of Big Data. The ultimate goal of dealing with Big Data is to derive actionable insights, make informed decisions, and create value. Organizations invest in Big Data technologies and analytics to turn this wealth of information into an asset.

9.2 Big Data Technologies

The era of Big Data has ushered in a plethora of technologies designed to handle the massive volume, velocity, variety, and complexity of data. These technologies enable organizations to collect, store, process, analyze, and extract insights from data on an unprecedented scale.

1. Hadoop: The Distributed Data Processing Framework

Hadoop is one of the foundational technologies in the world of Big Data. It's an open-source, distributed computing framework that allows for the storage and processing of vast amounts of data across clusters of commodity hardware. Hadoop's core components include the Hadoop Distributed File System (HDFS) for storage and the MapReduce programming model for data processing. It provides scalability, fault tolerance, and the ability to work with structured and unstructured data.

2. Spark: In-Memory Data Processing

Apache Spark is another prominent distributed computing framework designed for Big Data processing. What sets Spark apart is its in-memory processing capabilities, which make it significantly faster than Hadoop's MapReduce. Spark supports a wide range of data processing tasks, including batch processing, stream processing, machine learning, and graph processing.

3. NoSQL Databases: Flexible Data Storage

Traditional relational databases struggle to handle the volume and variety of data encountered in Big Data scenarios. NoSQL (Not Only SQL) databases offer a flexible and scalable alternative. Types of

NoSQL databases include document stores (e.g., MongoDB), key-value stores (e.g., Redis), column-family stores (e.g., Cassandra), and graph databases (e.g., Neo4j). These databases are well-suited for storing unstructured and semi-structured data.

4. Data Warehouses: Structured Data Analytics

Data warehouses are specialized databases optimized for querying and reporting on structured data. They are used for business intelligence and data analytics. Some popular data warehousing solutions include Amazon Redshift, Google BigQuery, and Snowflake. These platforms offer fast query performance and support SQL-based analytics.

5. Apache Kafka: Real-Time Data Streaming

Apache Kafka is a distributed streaming platform designed to handle real-time data streams at scale. It allows organizations to collect, process, and analyze data in real-time, making it essential for applications like IoT, clickstream analysis, and log aggregation.

6. Machine Learning and AI Tools: Extracting Insights

Machine learning and artificial intelligence (AI) play a pivotal role in extracting insights from Big Data. Tools and libraries like TensorFlow, PyTorch, scikit-learn, and Apache Mahout enable organizations to build predictive models, conduct sentiment analysis, perform image recognition, and more. These technologies enhance decision-making and enable automation based on data-driven insights.

7. Cloud Computing Platforms: Scalable Infrastructure

Cloud providers such as Amazon Web Services (AWS), Microsoft Azure, and Google Cloud Platform offer scalable infrastructure for Big Data workloads. Organizations can easily provision and manage clusters, storage, and analytics services without the need for extensive on-premises hardware and maintenance.

8. Data Lakes: Unified Data Storage

Data lakes provide a centralized repository for storing and managing diverse data types, including structured, semi-structured, and unstructured data. Technologies like AWS S3, Azure Data Lake Storage, and Hadoop HDFS enable organizations to store massive volumes of data in a cost-effective and scalable manner.

9. Data Integration and ETL Tools: Data Pipeline Management

Extract, Transform, Load (ETL) tools and data integration platforms help organizations ingest, clean, and transform data from various sources into a format suitable for analysis. Tools like Apache NiFi, Talend, and Apache Beam facilitate data movement and transformation.

10. Data Visualization Tools: Communicating Insights

Data visualization tools like Tableau, Power BI, and D3.js allow organizations to create interactive and informative visualizations that make complex data more understandable. Visualization is crucial for communicating insights to stakeholders and decision-makers.

In the dynamic landscape of Big Data technologies, staying up-to-date with the latest tools and platforms is essential for organizations seeking to harness the full potential of their data. The choice of technology depends on the specific use case, data characteristics, and organizational goals, making it crucial to tailor the tech stack to fit the unique challenges posed by Big Data.

9.3 Hadoop and MapReduce

Hadoop and MapReduce are two foundational technologies in the world of Big Data. They emerged as game-changers, allowing organizations to process and analyze massive datasets in a distributed and scalable manner.

Hadoop: The Distributed Data Storage and Processing Framework

Hadoop is an open-source, distributed computing framework designed to address the challenges posed by Big Data. It was inspired by a research paper from Google on the Google File System (GFS) and the MapReduce programming model.

Key Components of Hadoop:

1. **Hadoop Distributed File System (HDFS):** HDFS is Hadoop's storage component. It is designed to store vast amounts of data across a distributed cluster of commodity hardware. HDFS divides data into blocks and replicates them across nodes for fault tolerance.
2. **MapReduce:** MapReduce is Hadoop's processing engine. It allows users to write programs that process large datasets in parallel across a distributed cluster. The "Map" phase processes data in parallel across nodes, and the "Reduce" phase aggregates and summarizes the results.
3. **YARN (Yet Another Resource Negotiator):** YARN is the resource management layer of Hadoop. It manages and allocates resources (CPU, memory) to various applications running on the Hadoop cluster. YARN enables multi-tenancy, allowing different workloads to coexist on the same cluster.

How MapReduce Works:

MapReduce is a programming model and processing engine that simplifies the distributed processing of data. Here's how it works:

1. **Map Phase:** In the Map phase, data is divided into smaller chunks, and each chunk is processed independently by a Map task. The output of the Map tasks is a set of key-value pairs, where the key is typically a data attribute, and the value is some derived information.
2. **Shuffle and Sort Phase:** After the Map phase, the key-value pairs are shuffled and sorted based on their keys. This phase ensures that all values associated with a particular key end up together.
3. **Reduce Phase:** In the Reduce phase, the sorted key-value pairs are processed by Reduce tasks. Each Reduce task handles a

unique key and its associated values, allowing for aggregation, summarization, or further processing.

Significance of Hadoop and MapReduce:

Hadoop and MapReduce have had a profound impact on Big Data processing for several reasons:

1. **Scalability:** Hadoop clusters can scale horizontally by adding more commodity hardware, making them suitable for handling the ever-increasing volume of data.
2. **Fault Tolerance:** Hadoop provides built-in fault tolerance. If a node fails during processing, the framework automatically redistributes tasks to other nodes, ensuring job completion.
3. **Cost-Effective Storage:** HDFS offers a cost-effective way to store and manage large datasets compared to traditional storage solutions.
4. **Parallel Processing:** MapReduce allows for parallel processing, reducing the time required to analyze massive datasets.
5. **Ecosystem:** The Hadoop ecosystem has expanded to include a wide range of tools and libraries for data ingestion, processing, and analysis, such as Hive (SQL-like querying), Pig (data flow scripting), and HBase (NoSQL database).

While Hadoop and MapReduce remain significant, newer technologies like Apache Spark have gained popularity due to their in-memory processing capabilities, which make them faster for certain types of workloads. However, Hadoop continues to be a foundational technology in the Big Data landscape, especially for organizations dealing with large-scale data storage and batch processing.

9.4 Apache Spark

Apache Spark is a powerful, open-source, distributed computing framework designed for Big Data processing. It has gained immense popularity in the field of data analytics due to its speed, versatility, and support for a wide range of data processing tasks.

Key Features of Apache Spark:

1. **In-Memory Processing:** One of Spark's standout features is its ability to perform in-memory processing. It keeps data in RAM, reducing the need to read from and write to disk, which significantly speeds up data processing tasks.
2. **Versatility:** Spark supports various data processing tasks, including batch processing, real-time streaming, machine learning, graph processing, and SQL queries. This versatility makes it a valuable tool for a wide range of use cases.
3. **Ease of Use:** Spark provides high-level APIs in multiple programming languages, including Scala, Python, Java, and R. It also includes libraries like Spark SQL and MLlib, which simplify data manipulation and machine learning tasks.
4. **Fault Tolerance:** Similar to Hadoop, Spark offers fault tolerance. It can recover from node failures and continue processing without data loss.

Core Components of Apache Spark:

1. **Spark Core:** This is the foundational component of Spark, providing the basic functionality for task scheduling, memory management, and fault recovery. It also includes the Resilient Distributed Dataset (RDD), a fundamental data structure in Spark.
2. **Spark SQL:** Spark SQL allows you to execute SQL queries on structured data, making it easier to work with structured data sources and integrate Spark with existing databases.
3. **Spark Streaming:** Spark Streaming enables real-time data processing by ingesting and processing data in micro-batches. It is particularly useful for real-time analytics, monitoring, and event-driven applications.
4. **MLlib (Machine Learning Library):** MLlib is Spark's machine learning library, offering a wide range of algorithms and tools for machine learning and statistical analysis. It simplifies the development of machine learning pipelines.
5. **GraphX:** GraphX is a graph processing library for Spark. It provides tools for graph analysis and computation, making it

suitable for tasks like social network analysis and recommendation systems.

Spark in Action:

Here are some common use cases where Spark excels:

- **Data ETL (Extract, Transform, Load):** Spark can efficiently handle data extraction, transformation, and loading tasks, making it valuable for data preparation.
- **Streaming Analytics:** Spark Streaming is used for real-time analytics in applications like fraud detection, network monitoring, and social media sentiment analysis.
- **Machine Learning:** MLlib simplifies the development of machine learning models, enabling predictive analytics and recommendation systems.
- **Interactive Analytics:** Spark SQL enables interactive querying and data exploration, which is valuable for ad-hoc analysis.
- **Graph Analytics:** GraphX is used for analyzing and processing large-scale graph data.

Advantages of Apache Spark:

- **Speed:** Spark's in-memory processing significantly improves processing speed compared to disk-based systems like Hadoop MapReduce.
- **Ease of Use:** High-level APIs and libraries simplify development, making it accessible to data engineers and data scientists.
- **Unified Platform:** Spark provides a unified platform for batch processing, real-time streaming, machine learning, and graph processing, reducing the need for multiple tools.
- **Community and Ecosystem:** Spark has a vibrant open-source community and a rich ecosystem of extensions and libraries.

CHAPTER 10: DATA SCIENCE IN PRACTICE

10.1 Case Studies and Projects

The Power of Practical Experience:

Imagine you're learning to play a musical instrument or mastering a sport. While theory and instruction manuals are valuable, nothing compares to the knowledge and skills gained through practice. The same holds true for data science. Case studies and projects offer an opportunity to apply what you've learned, hone your abilities, and tackle real-world data problems.

Why Case Studies and Projects Matter:

1. **Hands-On Learning:** Case studies and projects provide a hands-on learning experience. They take you beyond theoretical knowledge and immerse you in the practical aspects of data science.
2. **Problem-Solving Skills:** Data science is about solving complex problems. By working on case studies and projects, you develop problem-solving skills that are crucial in any data-driven role.
3. **Application of Techniques:** You get to apply data analysis, machine learning, and data visualization techniques to real data.

This practical application reinforces your understanding of these methods.

4. **Building a Portfolio:** A portfolio of completed projects showcases your abilities to potential employers or collaborators. It serves as evidence of your skills and can significantly boost your career prospects.

5. **Building Confidence:** Successfully completing projects boosts your confidence in your data science abilities. It's a tangible reminder that you can tackle challenging tasks and produce valuable insights.

Types of Case Studies and Projects:

1. **Exploratory Data Analysis (EDA):** EDA projects involve exploring datasets to understand their characteristics, uncover patterns, and identify potential areas of interest. EDA is the foundation for data-driven decision-making.

2. **Predictive Modeling:** Build models to make predictions or classifications. This could involve predicting sales, customer churn, or sentiment analysis on social media data.

3. **Recommendation Systems:** Create recommendation algorithms that suggest products, movies, or content to users based on their preferences and behavior.

4. **Natural Language Processing (NLP):** Analyze and process text data, including sentiment analysis, text classification, and language generation.

5. **Image and Computer Vision:** Develop models for image recognition, object detection, or medical image analysis.

6. **Time Series Analysis:** Analyze time-stamped data to make predictions or understand trends, common in finance, IoT, and weather forecasting.

7. **Big Data Projects:** Tackle large-scale data processing and analysis using tools like Hadoop, Spark, and NoSQL databases.

Tips for Successful Case Studies and Projects:

- **Start Small:** If you're new to practical data science, begin with manageable projects before tackling more complex ones.

- **Define Clear Objectives:** Clearly define the goals and objectives of your project. What problem are you trying to solve? What insights are you seeking?
- **Data Quality Matters:** Ensure data quality and perform data preprocessing as needed. Clean, well-structured data is critical for meaningful results.
- **Document Your Work:** Maintain detailed documentation of your project, including code, methodologies, and results. This documentation will be valuable for future reference.
- **Collaborate and Seek Feedback:** Collaboration with peers or mentors can provide valuable insights and feedback. Don't hesitate to seek guidance.

10.2 Best Practices

1. Clearly Define Objectives and Scope:

Before diving into a data science project, it's essential to have a clear understanding of the project's objectives and scope. What problem are you trying to solve? What questions are you seeking to answer? Defining these aspects upfront helps you stay focused and ensures that your efforts align with the project's goals.

2. Data Quality Assessment and Preprocessing:

Data is the lifeblood of data science, and its quality can significantly impact your results. Conduct a thorough data quality assessment to identify missing values, outliers, and inconsistencies. Address data preprocessing tasks such as cleaning, normalization, and feature engineering to prepare the data for analysis.

3. Exploratory Data Analysis (EDA):

Exploratory Data Analysis is a critical phase where you explore and understand the data's characteristics. Visualizations, summary statistics, and data profiling techniques reveal patterns, outliers, and potential insights. EDA guides your decisions on data transformations and modeling approaches.

4. Feature Selection and Engineering:

Feature selection involves choosing the most relevant variables for your modeling task. Feature engineering entails creating new features or transforming existing ones to improve model performance. These steps can significantly impact the quality of your predictive models.

5. Model Selection and Evaluation:

Selecting the right machine learning algorithm or modeling technique is vital. Evaluate models using appropriate metrics (e.g., accuracy, precision, recall, F1-score) and consider techniques like cross-validation to assess performance robustly. Avoid overfitting, which occurs when a model performs well on training data but poorly on unseen data.

6. Effective Data Visualization:

Data visualization is a powerful tool for conveying insights. Create clear, informative visualizations that help stakeholders understand the data and your findings. Use appropriate charts, graphs, and dashboards to communicate your results effectively.

7. Interpretability and Explainability:

Incorporate model interpretability and explainability into your workflow, especially when working on critical applications. Understand how your models arrive at decisions and be able to explain their predictions to non-technical stakeholders.

8. Collaboration and Communication:

Effective collaboration with domain experts, stakeholders, and team members is key. Maintain open lines of communication to ensure that your data science efforts align with the organization's goals and objectives.

9. Reproducibility and Documentation:

Document your work thoroughly. Maintain detailed records of data sources, preprocessing steps, model configurations, and results. Reproducibility ensures that others can replicate your work, verify your findings, and build upon your research.

10. Ethics and Privacy:

Data ethics and privacy should always be at the forefront of your data science projects. Respect data privacy regulations, avoid biased models, and be transparent about data usage.

11. Continuous Learning and Adaptation:

The field of data science is dynamic, with new techniques and technologies emerging regularly. Commit to continuous learning to stay current with best practices and evolving trends.

12. Deployment and Monitoring:

Translating your models into practical solutions is a crucial step. Deploy models in production environments, and establish monitoring mechanisms to track their performance over time. Continuously update models as new data becomes available.

13. Feedback and Iteration:

Data science projects rarely end with a single iteration. Embrace feedback from users and stakeholders to refine your models and improve outcomes. Be prepared to iterate on your work to achieve better results.

14. Project Management:

Effective project management practices, such as setting timelines, milestones, and priorities, are essential for keeping data science projects on track. Tools like project management software can be invaluable for coordination.

By incorporating these best practices into your data science projects, you'll enhance your ability to deliver meaningful insights, solve complex problems, and contribute value to your organization. The practical application of these principles will help you navigate the complexities of real-world data science with confidence and competence.

10.3 Ethical Considerations

1. Data Privacy and Security:

Protecting the privacy and security of individuals' data is paramount. Always adhere to data privacy laws and regulations, such as the General Data Protection Regulation (GDPR) in Europe or the Health Insurance Portability and Accountability Act (HIPAA) in the United States. Anonymize or pseudonymize sensitive data, implement robust access controls, and encrypt data when necessary.

2. Informed Consent:

When collecting data from individuals, ensure that you have their informed consent. Clearly communicate the purpose of data collection, how the data will be used, and provide options for individuals to opt out or withdraw their consent at any time.

3. Avoiding Bias and Discrimination:

Bias can inadvertently seep into data and models, leading to unfair and discriminatory outcomes. Regularly audit data for biases related to gender, race, age, and other sensitive attributes. Use fairness-aware machine learning techniques to reduce bias in models, and be transparent about any bias that remains.

4. Transparency and Explainability:

Maintain transparency in your data science processes. Be able to explain how models arrive at their predictions, and make this information accessible to stakeholders. Transparency builds trust and helps users understand and trust the results.

5. Responsible AI:

Artificial intelligence and machine learning models should be used responsibly. Avoid deploying AI systems that can harm individuals or make decisions with significant consequences without human oversight. Develop and enforce guidelines for ethical AI use.

6. Data Governance:

Implement robust data governance practices within your organization. This includes clear data ownership, data stewardship, and data access policies. Ensure that data is used only for legitimate purposes and that unauthorized access is prevented.

7. Social Responsibility:

Consider the broader social implications of your work. Evaluate how your data science projects may impact society, communities, and individuals. Strive to use data science for the betterment of society and avoid harmful or unethical applications.

8. Accountability:

Accept responsibility for the consequences of your data science work. Be prepared to rectify errors or biases in models, and report any unethical practices or concerns to appropriate authorities within your organization.

9. Continuous Learning and Compliance:

Stay informed about evolving data ethics regulations and guidelines. Participate in ethics training and encourage ethical behavior among colleagues. Ensure that your data science practices align with the latest ethical standards.

10. Data Retention and Deletion:

Only retain data for as long as necessary for the stated purpose. Establish protocols for securely deleting data that is no longer needed to reduce the risk of data breaches or misuse.

11. Ethical Dilemmas and Whistleblowing:

Be prepared to address ethical dilemmas that may arise in your work. If you encounter unethical behavior within your organization, consider whistleblowing mechanisms that allow you to report such behavior anonymously.

12. Cross-Functional Collaboration:

Work closely with legal experts, ethicists, and domain specialists to navigate complex ethical questions. Collaborative decision-making can help ensure that ethical considerations are well-balanced with project objectives.

Incorporating ethical considerations into your data science practice is not just a legal or compliance requirement; it's a moral obligation. Ethical data science not only protects individuals' rights but also fosters trust, integrity, and responsible innovation in the field. By following ethical guidelines, data scientists can contribute positively to society while achieving meaningful results.

CHAPTER 11: CAREERS IN DATA SCIENCE

11.1 Data Science Roles

1. Data Analyst:

Responsibilities: Data analysts focus on extracting insights from data through exploratory data analysis (EDA) and visualization. They clean and prepare data, create reports and dashboards, and provide data-driven recommendations.

Skills: Proficiency in data analysis tools (e.g., SQL, Excel), data visualization (e.g., Tableau, Power BI), and statistical analysis.

2. Data Scientist:

Responsibilities: Data scientists are problem solvers who use data to answer complex questions. They develop machine learning models, conduct predictive and prescriptive analytics, and extract actionable insights from data.

Skills: Strong programming skills (e.g., Python, R), machine learning expertise, data preprocessing, and domain knowledge.

3. Machine Learning Engineer:

Responsibilities: Machine learning engineers focus on designing, building, and deploying machine learning models into production. They work closely with data scientists to implement and optimize algorithms.

Skills: Proficiency in machine learning frameworks (e.g., TensorFlow, PyTorch), software engineering, and deployment pipelines.

4. Data Engineer:

Responsibilities: Data engineers are responsible for collecting, storing, and managing data. They design data pipelines, create data warehouses, and ensure data availability and reliability.

Skills: Knowledge of big data technologies (e.g., Hadoop, Spark), database management, and data integration.

5. Business Intelligence (BI) Analyst:

Responsibilities: BI analysts focus on translating data into insights that inform business decisions. They create interactive dashboards, monitor KPIs, and provide stakeholders with actionable information.

Skills: Proficiency in BI tools (e.g., Tableau, QlikView), SQL, and data visualization.

6. Statistician:

Responsibilities: Statisticians use statistical methods to analyze data and draw meaningful conclusions. They design experiments, conduct hypothesis testing, and provide statistical insights.

Skills: Advanced statistical knowledge, expertise in statistical software (e.g., R, SAS), and experimental design.

7. AI Research Scientist:

Responsibilities: AI research scientists focus on advancing the field of artificial intelligence. They conduct research, develop new algorithms, and publish findings in academic or industry journals.

Skills: Deep knowledge of AI and machine learning, research skills, and proficiency in programming languages.

8. Data Science Manager/Director:

Responsibilities: Data science managers and directors oversee data science teams, set strategy, and ensure that data initiatives align with organizational goals. They also manage budgets and resources.

Skills: Leadership, project management, and strong knowledge of data science principles.

9. Chief Data Officer (CDO):

Responsibilities: CDOs are responsible for an organization's data strategy, governance, and data-driven decision-making. They play a strategic role in leveraging data as a valuable asset.

Skills: Strong leadership, data governance expertise, and a deep understanding of the organization's industry.

10. Data Science Consultant:

Responsibilities: Data science consultants work independently or with consulting firms to provide data-driven solutions to clients. They often work on a variety of projects across different industries.

Skills: Problem-solving, client communication, and expertise in data science methodologies.

Each of these roles plays a vital part in the data science ecosystem, contributing to the organization's ability to harness the power of data for decision-making and innovation. As you progress in your data science career, you may find opportunities to specialize in a particular role or gain expertise that spans multiple roles, depending on your interests and goals.

11.2 Building Your Data Science Career

1. Define Your Goals:

Begin by defining your career goals and aspirations. Consider the type of work that excites you the most, whether it's data analysis, machine learning, data engineering, or a combination of these. Having clear goals will guide your learning and career choices.

2. Education and Skill Development:

Acquiring the right skills is crucial in data science. Depending on your background, you may need to pursue formal education, such as a bachelor's or master's degree in data science, computer science, or a related field. Online courses, bootcamps, and self-study resources can also be valuable for skill development.

3. Programming Proficiency:

Data science relies heavily on programming. Python and R are two of the most commonly used programming languages in the field. Become proficient in one or both of these languages and explore relevant libraries and frameworks.

4. Data Manipulation and Analysis:

Master data manipulation techniques using tools like SQL and Pandas. Learn how to clean, preprocess, and analyze data effectively, as these skills are fundamental to most data science roles.

5. Machine Learning and Statistics:

Gain a solid understanding of machine learning algorithms and statistical methods. Explore supervised and unsupervised learning techniques, and be comfortable with both the theory and practical implementation.

6. Data Visualization:

Data visualization is a powerful tool for communicating insights. Learn how to create informative and visually appealing charts and dashboards using tools like Matplotlib, Seaborn, or Tableau.

7. Projects and Portfolio:

Hands-on experience is invaluable. Work on personal or open-source projects that demonstrate your skills and problem-solving abilities. Create a portfolio that showcases your work, including code, visualizations, and project descriptions.

8. Networking:

Build a professional network by attending conferences, meetups, and online forums related to data science. Networking can lead to valuable connections, mentorship opportunities, and job referrals.

9. Internships and Entry-Level Positions:

Consider internships or entry-level positions to gain practical experience. These roles provide exposure to real-world data challenges and can be a stepping stone to more advanced positions.

10. Certifications:

Certifications can validate your skills and knowledge in specific areas of data science. Consider certifications in machine learning, data engineering, or cloud computing platforms like AWS or Azure.

11. Domain Expertise:

Develop expertise in a specific industry or domain, such as healthcare, finance, or e-commerce. Domain knowledge can set you apart and make you a valuable asset in that field.

12. Stay Informed:

Data science is a rapidly evolving field. Stay up-to-date with the latest trends, technologies, and research by reading books, research papers, blogs, and following industry news.

13. Soft Skills:

Effective communication, problem-solving, and teamwork are essential soft skills in data science. Cultivate these skills to collaborate effectively with colleagues and convey your findings to non-technical stakeholders.

14. Continuous Learning:

Commit to lifelong learning. The field of data science is dynamic, and new tools and techniques are constantly emerging. Be adaptable and open to learning new skills.

Building a data science career is a journey that requires dedication and continuous effort. As you progress, you may find opportunities to specialize in a particular area or pivot into a different role that aligns with your evolving interests and expertise. By combining technical skills with effective communication and a passion for data-driven insights, you can create a fulfilling and successful career in data science.

www.ingramcontent.com/pod-product-compliance
Lightning Source LLC
LaVergne TN
LVHW051745050326
832903LV00029B/2739